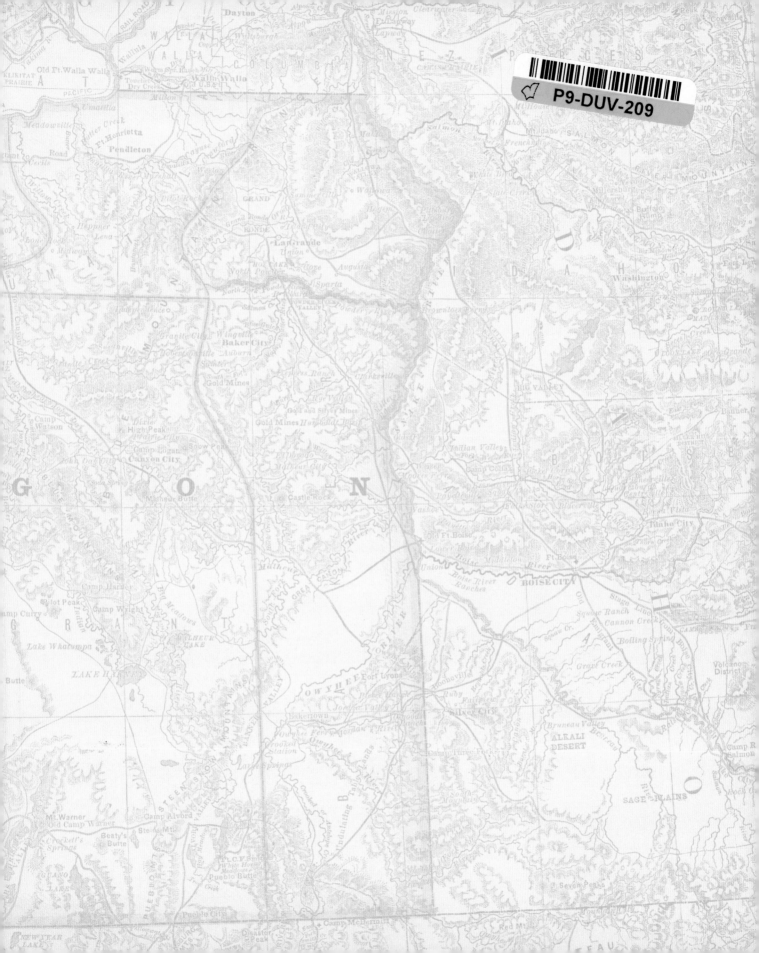

THE *Vintner's* KITCHEN

CELEBRATING THE WINES OF OREGON

THE *Vintner's* KITCHEN

CELEBRATING THE WINES OF OREGON

WILLIAM KING *&* RICK SCHAFER

arnica PUBLISHING, INC.
Portland, Oregon

Library of Congress Cataloging-in-Publication Data

King, William, 1952-
 The vintner's kitchen : celebrating the wines of Oregon / author, William King ; photographer, Rick Schafer.
   p. cm. -- (A chef's bounty cookbook series ; v. 2)
  ISBN 978-0-9794771-3-3 (alk. paper)
 1. Cookery--Oregon. 2. Cookery, American. 3. Wine and wine making--Oregon. I. Title.

TX715.K5337 2009
641.59795--dc22

2008026855

Pomegranate and Spice Braised Pork inspired in part by Pomegranate and Spice Braised Pork from SAN FRANCISCO CHRONICLE by Lynne Char Bennett. Copyright 2004 by San Francisco Chronicle. Reproduced with permission of San Francisco Chronicle in the format Other book via Copyright Clearance Center.

Braised Short Ribs of Beef inspired in part by Stout-Braised Short Ribs from Gourmet Magazine and epicurious.com. Copyright © March 2005. Reprinted with permission of US CondéNet.

Short Ribs Braised in Oregon Syrah inspired in part by Short Ribs Braised in Red Wine. Reprinted with the permission of Scribner, a division of Simon & Schuster Adult Publishing Group, from DANIEL BOULUD'S CAFÉ BOULUD COOKBOOK: FRENCH AMERICAN RECIPES FOR THE HOME COOK by Daniel Boulud and Dorie Greenspan. Copyright © 1999 by Daniel Boulud and Dorie Greenspan. All rights reserved.

Braised Lamb Shanks inspired in part by Braised Lamb Shanks from WELCOME TO MY KITCHEN by TOM VALENTI and ANDREW FRIEDMAN. Copyright © 2002 by Tom Valenti and Andrew Friedman. Reprinted by permission of HarperCollins Publishers.

Frangelico® Liqueur is a registered product of C&C International Ltd.

Lustau Sherry is a registered product of Emilio Lustau SA.

R.W. Knudsen Family® Organic Pear Juice is a registered product of Knudsen & Sons, Inc.

Tabasco® Pepper Sauce is a registered product of McIlhenny Company.

Tillamook® Cheese is a registered product of Tillamook Country Creamery Association (TCCA).

NOTICE: Consumption of raw meats and seafood may increase your risk of contracting food-borne illnesses.

Photography: Rick Schafer
Cover and text design: Aimee Genter and Emily Garcia

Editorial Team:

Gloria Martinez, *editor-in-chief*   Mattie Ivy, *project coordinator*
Rick Schafer, *creative director*   Teresa Schafer, *recipe testing, food stylist*
Dick Owsiany, *senior director of project development*   Michael Palodichuk, *research & editorial assistant*
Aimee Genter, *senior graphic designer*   Shannon Hunt, *research & editorial assistant*
Emily García, *junior graphic designer*   Kristin Eberman, *research & editorial assistant*

Arnica Publishing, Inc.
3880 SE Eighth Ave, Suite 110
Portland, Oregon 97202
Phone: (503) 225-9900
Fax: (503) 225-9901
www.arnicacreative.com

Arnica books are available at special discounts when purchased in bulk for premiums and sales promotions, as well as for fund-raising or educational use. Special editions or book excerption can also be created for specification. For details, contact the Sales Director at the address above.

My wife Jennifer and I are blessed with many wonderful friends. I dedicate this book to all of them for their immeasurable contributions to our love of life...and our love of wine!

—WILLIAM KING

william king would like to acknowledge...

The production of the *Chef's Bounty*™ books has been a labor of love for all of us. It is such a joy to chronicle the work of chefs and winemakers in our beautiful state of Oregon. And, in this case, it has been lots of fun to get to know the vintners, hear their stories, and share their favorite recipes. My thanks to all of the folks who were gracious enough to contribute their time, their culinary favorites, and their passion for making great wine.

A very special thanks to Susan Sokol Blosser for her contributions to the book, and to Oregon's world-class wine industry.

Thanks also to Cole Danehower for his help and the vast knowledge he provided all of us during the development and production of this book.

To the team at Arnica, thanks for all your expertise and efforts. Gloria Martinez, my editor and her team of graphic designers, Aimee Genter and Emily García, and editorial assistants, Mattie Ivy, Michael Palodichuk, and Shannon Hunt, who have created another beautiful book. To Dick Owsiany, Kristin Eberman, Matt Gerber, Ken Rowe, and Melva Manning for all their efforts in production, sales, and marketing. And to Mary Anderson, Rachael Turner and Troy Turner, for keeping us all moving in the right direction.

A special thank you to Ross Hawkins and Diane Vines for their support and commitment to the *Chef's Bounty*™ series and their dedication to telling Oregon's story.

Finally, my deep appreciation for and thanks to my friend and partner, Rick Schafer, who fills these books with beautiful photography that comes from his heart.

To the individuals and their families who pioneered the Oregon wine industry: The Sommers, Letts, Courys, Eraths, Adelsheims, Vuylstekes, Ponzis, Campbells, and the Sokol Blossers. Like a grape on a vine, thank you for planting the seeds and nurturing this industry in its infancy.

—RICK SCHAFER

rick schafer would like to acknowledge...

I would like to thank the wineries and their families that allowed us into their lives and shared with us the wonderful recipes that are in this book. In a continuation of the *Chef's Bounty*™ series, this is a celebration of agricultural families that represent Oregon. I have great respect for their hard work and passion.

Thank you to Jim Bernau, for his constant availability, and for sharing his vast knowledge of this industry as I researched this book.

Thank you to Jason Stoller Smith, for going out of his way to help us with preparing recipes for this book.

A very special thank you to Ross Hawkins and Diane Vines for their belief and support of this project: and a sincere debt of gratitude and appreciation to the management and staff of Arnica Publishing, Inc., for their quality of work.

Thanks to my wife Teresa and our children for putting up with another book project.

To my friend Bill King, whose passion for food and wine is exceeded only by his love for family and friends. A toast to you Bill: Live, Laugh, Love!

table of contents

foreword

by Susan Sokol Blosser

In the space of one generation, Oregon wines have gone from local oddity to international acclaim. With close to 400 wineries and 17,500 acres of wine grapes, Oregon has taken its place as one of the premier wine-producing regions of the world. Oregon wines are served at the White House, on the toniest cruise ships, and at the top Michelin-starred and Zagat-rated restaurants. They command top dollar and are sought out by wine connoisseurs worldwide.

Wine is often portrayed as a luxury to be served on special occasions. While that really expensive bottle may be saved for a holiday or birthday, winegrowers believe that wine is an important part of a meal and enhances the dining experience. Good food demands good wine, and vice-versa. Whether sharing with friends or just sitting down with the family, wine belongs on the dinner table.

Matching food and wine is a skill. Where do you begin? Do you start with the wine or the food? Chefs look at the dishes they create and wonder what wines will go well with them. Winemakers taste the wines they produce and wonder what foods should accompany them. Regardless of the approach, the idea is the same—wine and food go together. It takes experience to pair wine and food but it's an arena where practicing is the best part. *The Vintner's Kitchen* is here to help.

Oregon winegrowers are down-to-earth and unpretentious, pretty much focused on growing healthy, flavorful grapes and crafting wonderful wine. Don't be fooled by the jeans and fleece vests, the old cars and pickups, and the informal style. When it comes to food and wine, Oregon winegrowers are unexpectedly demanding, insisting on the very best. The wines on the table and the food chosen to go with them must be of the highest quality, the most delicious, the most carefully prepared. Wine and food is serious business. Traveling the U.S. to market and sell Oregon wine, winegrowers seek out the top establishments. As an Oregon winegrower, I believe my demands are simple, but representative: fresh, local, sustainably grown ingredients; creative menus; perfect preparation and seasoning; beautiful presentation; and, of course, excellent service.

Eating at home, our meals may be simpler, but our palates have been trained in the best restaurants and we demand the same quality. Some of us love to cook and take on intricate recipes that make others shudder. Some of us would rather spend our time and energy savoring the final product with our wine. No matter. For me and other Oregon winemakers, eating and drinking well is an endless pursuit. *The Vintner's Kitchen* reflects this passion. These are real recipes from Oregon wine families, some handed down over generations, others created to go with specific wines. They range from simple to complex, but in each case the wonderful products of Oregon take center stage and represent the diverse bounty of Oregon: vegetables, fruits and nuts, artisan cheeses, fish and shellfish, pork, lamb, beef, chicken, and dairy. An omnivore's delight. *Bon appétit!*

introduction

by William King

This book tells the story, it is the story of Oregon's wine industry, very new by European standards, yet as vibrant and dynamic as any wine-producing region in the world. It is the fascinating story of the people who left their "other" lives and pioneered wine making as a means to make a personal connection to the land in a productive, artistic, and quality-committed fashion. This is a tribute to those pioneers and to the people who followed in their footsteps and have helped to promote the growth of the Oregon wine industry over the past forty years.

The Vintner's Kitchen: Celebrating the Wines of Oregon, is a celebration—a celebration of celebrating! Why work so hard and dedicate so much time, energy, and money for any other reason than to reap the benefits of hard work and celebrate the success? Traditionally, wine is known as the beverage of celebration. The age-old ritual of opening, pouring, toasting, and drinking wonderful wines is emblematic of the milestones and celebrations of our lives. Those memorable occasions naturally include the enjoyment of great food designed to lead and/or follow the juice of the grapes, each complementing the other as vehicles for celebration.

This book is a guide intended to demystify and strip the pretense from personal enjoyment of wines. Too often, the complexities surrounding wine overshadow the simple pleasure of drinking a wonderful glass of wine. The growing regions…varietals…styles…labels…the science of growing the grapes, and the processes of making wine can be a seemingly endless and truly overwhelming litany of information. The vast differences in flavor profiles ranging from dramatic to extremely subtle are often too intimidating to identify. Wine stewards, shop owners, and sommeliers all function at a strata well above the knowledge level most of us enjoy. As for menu planning and pairings—whites with seafood…? Reds with meat…? But, which white with which seafood? For me, enjoying wine should be just that…an enjoyable experience. A little knowledge is helpful, so we'll cover the basics and keep it fun and interesting. Of course, there is really only one thing you need to know, and that is…What do you like?

Of course, this book is a cookbook. Wine and food are the most natural of partners. We'll bring you options for pairing with and cooking with the fabulous wines of Oregon. I have chosen some of my favorite personal recipes that suit a variety of occasions, cooking styles, and varying levels of culinary expertise. But the stars of this show are the recipes contributed by the owners, vintners, friends, and families of our region's best and most exciting wineries. These are recipes that have become part of their families' celebratory repertoire throughout generations. You will also find recipes from chefs designed specifically to highlight the outstanding characteristics of the winery's best vintage. It is my hope that you will discover new recipes that you will adopt and add to your menus as you celebrate the significant occasions of your life and honor the work of our region's dedicated, award-winning winemakers.

This beautiful state of Oregon is one of great culinary bounty, a region so luxuriously blessed with foods and wine that it almost defies description. This is the story of Oregon's regional wines and foods—the story of the vine, and the kitchen, and the people who bring this magnificent bounty together in celebration.

Here's to the pleasure of the table—from my kitchen and from the Vintner's Kitchen!

—Bill King

vintages

A Year in the Life of Oregon's Wine Industry
by William King

winter The wet cold days are "down time" in the vineyards. Holidays pass and the wineries and tasting rooms are, for the most part, quiet. But as winter enters its final weeks, activity begins as the crew at Willamette Valley Vineyards heads out for the critical task of pruning the vines. Experienced eyes select the canes best suited to bear this year's fruit, perhaps only two to four, plus a couple of spurs for next year's development are retained. This is long, slow work, especially in Willamette Valley's winter weather. Yet it is one of the most important times in the vineyard. The cycle has begun.

april Spring budbreak has begun as the vines open and begin the development that will produce this year's vintage. Nature must be kind as a surprise late frost can be disastrous. At Stoller Vineyards, Bill and Cathy are optimistic, as their south-facing vineyard slopes are usually free from potential damage. As with all agricultural crops, weather can make or break a vintage. Too cold in the spring, too wet in the fall, too hot in the summer—any of these conditions can dramatically affect the fragile Pinot noir grapes.

june Lynn and Ron Penner-Ash are more concerned about the unusually cold, wet weather than in most years. The vines have begun to flower and the tiny blossoms are at Nature's mercy. These will become the grape clusters, and cold, wet, windy weather can damage the flowers before they can "set" to form the berries. Nestled between the Chehalem Mountains and the Red Hills of Dundee, Penner-Ash Wine Cellars is blessed with a magnificent view of the northern Willamette Valley. From there, so much of our bounty is evidence of Nature's grace. Yet for a few weeks at this time each year, Nature can be more foe than friend. Hold your breath and pray for sun!

As the season begins – and as fears of cold, wet weather and potential for disaster fade, it is now time to take advantage of Summer's sun and warmth. At Ponzi Vineyards, the family is fully engaged in vineyard activities. Michel is managing the all-important process of trellising the newly developed vines. This step is critical to controlling the leaf canopy and allowing sunlight and air to reach the grape clusters. When properly managed, the fruit is also much easier to access and harvest in the fall.

the green harvest As summer and the development of the grapes progress, decisions are being made in the Ribbon Springs Vineyard at Adelsheim. Jack and Lynn Loacker's crew must select the best grape clusters, those with the best development and greatest potential for quality juice, and remove the other clusters that appear to be sub-par. This culling of green grapes reduces the load on the vines and directs all their energy toward the quality fruit. The goal: intensely flavored grapes and more interesting, high-quality Pinot.

all summer long

The constant focus on weather remains. At this point, warm, damp, cool nights, and no rain are the keys to a good, or even great, year. Response to conditions is a daily focus. To irrigate or not? Cultivation, hedging, pruning to ensure the ideal leaf canopy and perhaps some ongoing green harvest are all the processes that produce quality grapes at RoxyAnn Winery in Southern Oregon's Rogue Valley. Vineyard manager Jon Meadors performs all of these tasks within the guidelines of sustainable land management. Contrary to the generally held impression that Oregon is consistently wet, Oregon's summers are most typically hot and dry, and can last well into September or even early October. To me, it is the most perfect summer weather in the entire country. But for the vineyards, even this idyllic environment creates problems. And so it goes as the grapes begin to turn color and ripen—we're getting closer—harvest time is near!

late september, early october

The time is very near at Domaine Drouhin. Veronique Drouhin-Boss and her brother, Philippe Drouhin are watchful. They look and taste and track the weather forecast. Is it time? Can we get more out of the grapes? When will it rain? Scott Paul Wright has decided that today is the day. Scott Paul Wines will start their harvest! This is strictly hand work. In the very early morning, before the sun warms the vines, the crew is out. Quick decisions, fast hands, sharp shears. Row by row…precision and rhythm…bucket after bucket…into totes…fork lifts rolling and then on to the crusher-slammer, and then to the press—grapes to wine—this year's vintage is in.

the crush

Now the grapes make their way from fruit to juice. This must happen quickly, as the Pinot cannot sit. The crush releases the juice as the skins are broken and the must is removed to vats for fermentation where grape sugars convert to alcohol and juice to wine. As the must ferments, a "cap" of skins rise to the surface and is re-submerged periodically to extract color at the appropriate levels. The process is allowed to evolve for about two weeks, then the must is pressed to extract the very new, immature wine. Then the wine is drawn off to barrels or stainless for aging. The heavy work is done. The new wine will take its time to evolve…to greatness? Time and the impact of all the efforts in the vineyard and during the wine-making process will tell. It will be a few weeks, or many months before the wine is bottled. This year's vintage is ready to reach its potential. Winter has returned. In a couple of months "next year" will begin and the cycle of life for Oregon's wines will be renewed.

celebrating oregon wines

by Cole Danehower

In just forty years—the span of one working life—Oregon has gone from having no wine industry at all to being one of the globe's most prestigious wine growing regions. And yet even today, Oregon's remarkable wine story is often overshadowed by the glitz and allure of her neighbors to the south and north.

It is true that Oregon ranks third behind California and Washington in the number of wineries, and even further behind in terms of wine production. But wine in Oregon has never been about numbers, whether measuring size, volume, or critics' scores. Rather, here wine is about character and authenticity—about soul. Oregon wine has always been about the soul of the people who farm and make the wine as much as the soul of the places where the grapes are grown.

Simply put, Oregon's wine world is unique.

To fully appreciate Oregon's wine character, it is important to explore a few key themes that make Oregon's wine community—it doesn't seem quite right to call it an "industry"—special. The place to start is with Oregon itself.

oregon, the place for wine

When viewed from the vantage of a vintner, Oregon is two states. In the northwest portion, on the fringes of the vast Willamette Valley drainage, a series of rolling foothills containing varied volcanic and marine sedimentary soils present vistas of vinous opportunity. This is one state of Oregon wine—the cool-climate Oregon.

Southwest of Portland, in the sparse soils of the southerly and easterly facing slopes of the Dundee Hills, the Eola and Amity Hills, Ribbon Ridge and the Chehalem Mountains, and the foothills surrounding the tiny towns of Yamhill, Carlton, and the bigger burb of McMinnville, vineyards abound and Pinot predominates.

Standing in one of these vineyards, sweltering under the summer sun, it is hard to think of the area as cool, but to a wine grape, it is. At roughly 45°N latitude (famously, but perhaps irrelevantly similar to Burgundy—after all, Minneapolis shares the same latitude) and this close to the Pacific Ocean, the Willamette Valley's growing season is relatively short, with average summer temperatures lower than almost any other West Coast wine region. Not every grape variety is well suited to these climatic conditions, but those that are, thrive here.

On the one hand, grapes grown in this region are protected in the summer from the hurting heat of the valley floor because of their elevation (roughly between 200 and 800 feet). and the moderating marine air that sneaks in from the ocean through a few gaps in the Coast Range. Compatibly, these same grapes are protected in the winter from killing frosts because the cold air sloughs down the hills, and again because of the protective powers of the moist marine air.

Though the Willamette Valley hills offer beneficial vineyard sites, viticulture here is not without risk—Oregon's cool climate is, in fact, at the outer edge of viability for *vitis vinifera,* the European wine grape, and not every vintage is a sure thing. Frosts in the spring can occur as the vine begins its growth cycle, drastically diminishing crops. Rain in the fall can come early, before the grapes are fully ripe, rushing the harvest and threatening the quality of the vintage.

But when conditions are good, as they have mostly been in the last decade or so, Oregon's cool climate wine country can produce some of the best wines in the world.

But there is another, equally vital, Oregon wine state—the warm-climate Oregon. Extending south of Eugene, through the Hundred Valleys of the Umpqua around and to the north and west of Roseburg, further south through the Illinois, Applegate, and Rogue Valleys, all the way to the border with California, Southern Oregon is the largest of the state's warm-climate regions.

It is also—and this is frequently forgotten—the home of modern winegrowing in Oregon, the place where vitis vinifera was first planted. In 1961, at Hillcrest Vineyard in—as his wine labels said—"Oregon's Umpqua Valley," Richard Sommer planted Riesling and Cabernet sauvignon, soon followed by Chardonnay, Gewürztraminer, Semillon, Sauvignon blanc, Zinfandel—and Oregon's first Pinot noir.

This part of Oregon has a much more diverse topography than the Willamette Valley, making it more difficult to generalize accurately about growing conditions over the 2 million acres of the appellation. Nevertheless, the vineyard-supporting valleys of Southern Oregon generally receive more heat—in many places much more heat—thanks to both their more inland and southerly location. Cooling marine air is only a factor in the western reaches of the region, and none at all for the majority of vineyards.

Yet at the same time, the growing season can be shorter than the Willamette Valley, especially in the Rogue Valley appellation, because of the higher vineyard elevations, generally ranging from 900 feet to over 1800 feet. Spring and fall frosts can be a definite danger, and is an important limiting factor for winegrowers.

As is water. Southern Oregon is more arid than cool-climate Oregon. Rainfall is approximately ten inches less on average than the Willamette Valley, making irrigation and water dependability a critical winegrowing variable.

Similar warm-climate conditions exist in the Columbia Gorge along the Oregon-Washington border, where a vibrant winery scene has developed in recent years. From Hood River in the west to The Dalles in the east, vineyards experience warm and wet, to hot and arid conditions, depending on location, elevation, and exposure.

Continuing east, Oregon's hottest viticultural area can be found in the state's portion of the Walla Walla Valley appellation, near Milton-Freewater. Here summer temperatures can easily exceed 100° F, but winter temperatures can also drop well below zero, causing risk of winter kill. Even so, excellent growing conditions here have inspired an increasing number of vineyard and winery developments.

Oregon's distinctive set of clearly delineated wine countries means the state can successfully grow a full range of top-quality wine grapes. In cool-climate Oregon, Burgundian and Alsatian varieties prevail: Pinot noir, Pinot gris, Pinot blanc, Riesling, Chardonnay, Gewürztraminer. Warm-climate Oregon excels at Bordeaux, Rhône, and Spanish grapes: Merlot, Cabernet sauvignon, Syrah, Cabernet franc, Tempranillo, Viognier, and Albariño.

All those wonderful grape varieties grown throughout Oregon's wine countries have two particularly important flavor elements in common: great purity of fruit and vibrant natural acidity. This is no accident.

Long before there were wine grapes here, Oregon was famous for the quality of its fruits. Pears, apples, blackberries, sweet cherries, cranberries, raspberries, plums, boysenberries, loganberries, blueberries, strawberries, apricots, currants, and gooseberries all have a history of high-quality production in Oregon.

So why not wine grapes?

Starting in the 1960s Oregon's first generation of modern winegrowers began cultivating wine grapes. And from the beginning, these pioneers established an attitude that emphasized fruit quality as the foundation for wine quality. This stance has formed the entire history of Oregon's wine culture, and has resulted in an overall style for Oregon wines, from both climate regions, that makes them the ideal accompaniment to food.

The pioneers acted on an important observation well known to old-time fruit growers: you obtained the best varietal flavors from fruit whose normal point of optimum ripeness coincided with the natural end of the growing season. The Willamette Valley, they postulated, offered a climate that matched the natural growing pattern of Pinot noir, perhaps the most delicate and elegant of the noble wine grape varieties.

The idea of matching a specific wine grape variety to the particular conditions of a site or region in order to realize the best qualities of the fruit in the finished wine was not yet widely appreciated. That concept, though, was realized in Oregon.

Here, warm summer days are followed by cool nights, allowing for the even maturation of sugars and flavors while maintaining a healthy balance of natural acidity in the grapes. Just as the grapes are nearing their maximum level of development, the summer ends, cooler temperatures creep in, and the grapes reach balanced physiological ripeness with optimum flavor development.

Pinot noir was grown in California at the time, but with mixed results. The warm California weather tended to accelerate sugar development at an unnatural rate, leaping ahead of flavor maturation. When sugars reached the point where the grapes had to be picked—weeks before the end of the growing season—there was no longer time to wait for further growth in flavors. The resulting wines rarely captured the delicacy and fullness of true varietal character.

They do in Oregon.

Likewise in warm-climate Oregon, modern wine growers have discovered that the wide diurnal swings in temperature impart a crispness to their wines. The warm-to-hot days are perfect for maturing sugars in grapes adapted to a warmer climate, while the cool nights act as a brake on too rapid ripening, helping maintain an edge of acidity that ensures bright and fresh varietal flavors.

Whether an elegant Pinot noir, a succulent Syrah, an aromatic Viognier, an earthy Tempranillo, or a vivacious Riesling, Oregon's wines consistently reflect a clarity of correct fruit flavor reinforced by a vibrant, mouthwatering character. These are the kinds of wines chefs adore, and wine lovers savor.

A maxim of food and wine pairing is that "what grows together, goes together." Oregon is a supreme example of this. Our natural bounty of foods and ingredients provide classic matchings for the wines we grow.

Few would dispute that salmon and Pinot noir are a natural pairing, but equally compelling is Pinot noir with dishes made from Oregon's wild mushrooms and truffles. Halibut and steelhead are delightful with a crisp Pinot gris, but so are lightly toasted hazelnuts tossed in a salad with heirloom tomatoes. Fresh-from-the-sea oysters almost require a racy dry Oregon Riesling, but an unoaked Chardonnay, an uncommon Grüner Veltliner, or a zesty Albariño provide compelling local alternatives.

An excellent accompaniment to an Oregon-raised lamb shank can be found in any good Syrah from the Rogue Valley, or perhaps a Zinfandel from 100-year-old vines in the Columbia Gorge. Grass-fed beef from eastern Oregon is well enhanced by a rich Umpqua Valley Tempranillo, or a well balanced Bordeaux-style blend from the Applegate.

Is it any wonder that chefs from around the country envy the bounty we have here?

oregon, craft, commitment, and community

Recognizing the special qualities of Oregon as a place, our vintners routinely take steps to protect and improve their environment (both physical and social), the quality of their fruit, and the integrity of their wines. This also sets us apart from other wine regions.

It is interesting to note that Oregon has no big wineries. The largest ones (at around 120,000 cases annually) are miniscule when compared to the behemoths of California and Washington, where more than a few wine brands have yearly production measured in the millions of cases. The average Oregon winery makes less than 5,000 cases per year. It is common to find wines of which only a few hundred cases were made—frequently even less than that.

And these wines, indeed, almost every wine made in Oregon, is hand-crafted. Vines are pruned, shoot-thinned, and leaf-pulled by hand—on average, each vine gets "touched" by a worker from three to eight times during its growing season. At harvest, grape clusters are individually inspected, manually cut, and laboriously hauled from the vine rows in forty-pound bins. In most wineries, grapes are sorted by hand, and ferments are monitored around the clock. Such attention to detail is not strictly necessary, but the added commitment helps ensure only the highest quality fruit is made into Oregon wine.

Oregon also has almost no corporately-owned wineries; the vast majority of the state's 400-plus wineries are family enterprises, many in the second generation of ownership and winemaking. Most were (and still are) started on a shoestring, limping through years of building customer loyalty before finding financial success. Yet these small businesses today cumulatively contribute over $1.4 billion in total economic impact to Oregon.

Consistent with the private ownership of Oregon's wineries is the unusually independent spirit of the state's winemakers, winegrowers, and winery owners. From the beginning, Oregon's wine community was built by freethinkers pursuing distinctly personal wine ambitions. This maverick ethos resulted in the planting of grape varieties in places where conventional wisdom said they would not thrive (Willamette Valley Pinot noir and Pinot gris in the 1960s and 1970s, for example) and in the production of wine varieties that had never been seen in the Northwest before (Southern Oregon Tempranillo in the 1990s and Grüner Veltliner in the early 2000s).

Yet this independence is tempered by attention to communal good. Early on, Oregon's winemakers understood the value of protecting what they were building. They agreed to fund viticultural research and industry marketing by imposing on themselves the steepest wine industry self-tax in the country. They also pushed for, and enacted, the nation's strictest state wine labeling laws to ensure a high level of wine quality and reliable integrity for consumers. Consistent with that ethic, and the desire to pass on to future generations a healthy wine ecosystem, Oregon has been a pioneer in sustainable, organic, and biodynamic viticulture.

Sokol-Blosser Winery was the first winery in the nation to receive a Leadership in Energy and Environmental Design (LEED®) certification from the U.S. Green Building Council, and Stoller Vineyards was the first Gold LEED® Certified winery in the country. Oregon's Low Input Viticulture & Enology (LIVE) program was the country's first sustainable certification agency for winegrowers, and Oregon-based Demeter Certified Biodynamic® is the nation's leading biodynamic certification program.

Oregon wineries also strive to give back to their communities. ¡Salud! is a unique, winery-funded program that provides health care services to seasonal vineyard farm workers. Supported each year by a major auction and dinner fundraiser, ¡Salud! provides healthcare access to over 3,000 workers each year. Similarly, wineries donate their time and wine in support of Morrison Child and Family Services through the popular Cooking for Kids fundraising program.

All of these attitudes help make Oregon wine special.

oregon *terroir*

"Terroir" is a popular wine concept. Put simply, it means that a wine will reflect the unique conditions—soil, weather, elevation, sunlight—that are inherent to the place where the grapes were grown. I believe Oregon has a *terroir* of its own, a *terroir* that transcends the individual characteristics of any one vineyard site and reflects the wine character of the state as a whole.

Oregon's *terroir* is not just the sum of all the natural variables that go into defining a wine—the climate, the soils, the grape varieties, and the winemaking conditions. It is also the sum of all the people involved in producing Oregon's wine—the sustainable commitment of the winegrowers, the craft focus of the winemakers, the quality orientation of the winery owners, the hard labor of the vineyard workers…and the appreciation of the wine consumers.

This Oregon *terroir* is unique—it cannot be duplicated in any other place. It is inherent in the soil and the spirit of the vines and the people who comprise the Oregon wine community.

Let's celebrate the Oregon *terroir*. Let's open some Oregon wine!

---

cole danehower is co-publisher and editor-in-chief of *Northwest Palate,* the leading consumer magazine covering wine, food, and culinary travel in Oregon, Washington, British Columbia, and Idaho. He has been writing about Oregon and Pacific Northwest wine since 1998 when he created the *Oregon Wine Report* newsletter. In 2004 Cole was the recipient of a coveted James Beard Foundation Journalism Award for his Oregon wine writing.

Cole is a frequent wine judge (*Dallas Morning News,* Portland Indie Wine Festival, Oregon State Fair, Northwest Wine Summit, and others), has been the Oregon correspondent for *Wines & Vines* magazine and *AppellationAmerica,* and has had his food and wine writing published in *The Oregonian, The San Francisco Chronicle* the *Eugene-Register Guard, Wines and Vines,* and numerous other print and online venues.

Cole is currently writing a book, tentatively titled *Wine Countries of the Pacific Northwest—A Guide to the Wines, People, Places, and Vines of Washington, Oregon, British Columbia and Idaho,* planned for publication in early 2010.

appetizers

Whether it be for cocktail party hors d'oeuvres, a casual dinner, first course, or an elaborate multi-course meal, this section gets things started with Northwest style and a little something special for everyone's taste.

avocado crostini

from Reustle-Prayer Rock Vineyard and Winery

A simple yet rich and delicious hors d'oeuvre, this has become Reustle-Prayer Rock's signature appetizer. Ripe, yet firm avocados and a full-flavored Oregon chevre with a great French baguette or artisan loaf, and a bottle of unique and exotic grüner veltliner from Reustle-Prayer Rock Vineyards are all you need.

Serves 4

1 loaf artisan bread, sliced to 1/4-inch
About 4 tablespoons olive oil
1 package chèvre
1 large, ripe Haas avocado, thinly sliced
Sea salt
Freshly ground black pepper

Preheat the oven to 400°F.

Allow the cheese to reach room temperature, or microwave for 10 seconds to soften. Brush both sides of the bread with olive oil. Bake until crispy, and allow to cool. Spread a thin layer of chèvre on top of the prepared crostini. Top with the avocado slices and fan across crostini. Drizzle with olive oil. Season to taste with salt and pepper. Serve immediately.

about reustle-prayer rock vineyards

Reustle-Prayer Rock Vineyards is the first winery in the United States offering one of Austria's most exotic white wines—grüner veltliner. This wine is known for its remarkable tastes of white pepper, all sorts of citrus, and tropical fruits. It is a dry, weighty white with aging potential.

WINE PAIRING
Dobbes Family Estate
2007 Viognier

razor clam crostini

from Nick's Italian Cafe

Usually razor clams are prepared very simply by lightly seasoning and coating them, and then they are quickly sautéed or pan-fried. Here, we have a very different and delicious approach from Nick's Italian Café that combines them with a number of aromatics, chilled and chopped as a topping for crostini. Unique and very tasty!

Serves 8

5 pounds razor clams in shell
2 tablespoons unsalted butter
Extra virgin olive oil
1 onion, julienne
5 cloves garlic, peeled, halved
1/2 bunch fresh thyme
7 dried chilies, broken into halves
1 lemon (Using a vegetable peeler, remove zest in wide strips, and reserve the lemon for juicing.)

1/2 bottle dry white wine
2 small spring onions, finely diced
3 spears green garlic, finely diced
Kosher salt
Freshly cracked black pepper
1 artisan baguette

Begin by preparing a liquid in which to steam open the razor clams. Heat a large sauté pan, and melt together the butter and 3 tablespoons of olive oil. Lightly sauté the julienned onion and garlic cloves until the onion has sweated and the cloves have faintly started to brown. Add the thyme, chilies, and lemon zest, then carefully pour in the white wine. Steep this mixture until the alcohol has been boiled out of the wine (a few minutes). Using a slotted spoon, remove the solid ingredients from the pan, leaving only the steaming liquid.

Add the razor clams to the pan and remove as they open. Reserve 3 tablespoons of the cooking liquid, and allow the clams to cool before proceeding. Using a sharp paring knife, clean the clams by running the tip of the blade down the flesh of the clam and scrape away any debris. Chop the clam meat into a 1/4-inch dice and refrigerate.

Sauté the spring onions and green garlic in olive oil until tender. Chill the mixture in the refrigerator before proceeding.

Combine the chilled clam meat, onion and garlic mixture, and the reserved cooking liquid in a mixing bowl. Dress with extra virgin olive oil, lemon juice, kosher salt, and freshly ground black pepper to taste. Refrigerate.

Preheat the oven to 450°F.

While the crostini topping is chilling, prepare the crostini. Slice a fresh baguette on a slight bias approximately 1/4-inch wide. Lay the slices out on a baking sheet and drizzle generously with extra virgin olive oil and sprinkle with salt. Bake for 6 minutes or to desired crispness.

Allow the crostini to cool, and top with steamed clams. Serve paired with a fresh salad dressed simply with lemon, olive oil and salt.

arugula with truffle vinaigrette
and truffle-oil coated seastack triple cream cheese

from the Joel Palmer House

Here's a wonderful, simple way to resolve a decision on an appetizer or salad course using the beautiful Oregon truffle oil produced by Jack Czarnecki of the Joel Palmer House, one of the pre-eminent restaurants in the Willamette Valley wine country. Jack is one of the true experts on the subject of the wild mushrooms and truffles that are foraged in our region. He has just begun production of this luscious oil.

Serves 4

3 cups loosely packed arugula leaves
2 teaspoons balsamic vinegar
3 tablespoons Oregon white truffle oil
8 ounces triple cream-style cheese, such as Seastack from Port Townsend Creamery
12 (1/3-inch-thick) diagonal-cut baguette slices

Toss the arugula with the vinegar and 2 ounces of the truffle oil. Arrange on four plates a little off to the side. Place 2 ounces of cheese on each plate, pouring the rest of the truffle oil over the cheese, and serve with the baguette slices.

"Wine has been a part of civilized life for some seven thousand years. It is the only beverage that feeds the body, soul and spirit of man and at the same time stimulates the mind...."

—ROBERT MONDAVI, *Harvests of Joy*

crostini

with rogue creamery blue cheese, wildflower honey, and oregon hazelnuts

from RoxyAnn Winery

The crisp acidity of a RoxyAnn Pinot Gris pairs well with the creamy richness of this appetizer.

Serves 4

12 (1/3-inch-thick) diagonal-cut baguette slices
3 ounces Rogue Creamery Blue cheese, at room
    temperature (or Gorgonzola or Roquefort)
1/2 cup coarsely chopped toasted, husked hazelnuts
Local wildflower honey

Preheat the oven to 400°F.

Place the baguette slices in single layer on a baking sheet. Toast in the oven until golden, about 8 minutes. (This can be made 4 hours ahead.)

Spread the blue cheese on the baguette slices. Sprinkle hazelnuts over each. Drizzle each slice lightly with honey, and serve on tray.

gougères

from Chehalem

The recipe for these small, savory French hors d'oeuvres came to the Peterson-Nedry family from a dear friend, Linda Young Baldwin. Linda made them for a dinner party at her home, and it was love at first bite. These make a perfect light start with a crisp white or sparkler.

Serves 8 as an appetizer

1 cup water
1/2 cup butter (1 stick)
1 cup all-purpose flour
4 eggs
1 1/2 cups grated Gruyère cheese
1 teaspoon Dijon mustard
1/2 teaspoon salt
1 teaspoon dry mustard
Dash of Tabasco® Pepper Sauce, or a pinch of cayenne pepper

Preheat the oven to 450°F.

Bring the water and butter to a boil in a medium-sized pan. Using a wooden spoon, stir in the flour all at once and beat until the mixture forms a large, smooth clump. Remove from the heat and beat in the eggs, one at a time, using an electric mixer, and mixing thoroughly between each addition. Add the cheese, mustard, salt, dry mustard, and pepper sauce, and mix well.

Drop heaping teaspoons of the batter onto a large baking sheet forming a circle or "wreath." Once the circle is formed, drop additional spoonfuls between the original drops.

Bake for 10 minutes, then reduce the heat to 350°F and continue baking for 10 minutes longer. Finally, reduce the heat to 325°F, and bake for 15 additional minutes. The ring should be puffy and brown. Remove the pan from the oven and immediately prick the gougères on their sides or bottoms with a toothpick or a fork, so that the steam can escape.

Chef's note: Gougères may be baked separately as small puffs. Reduce the cooking time, and watch them carefully so they don't burn.

gougères

from Chef William King

This is my favorite simple hors d'oeuvre, especially for pre-function red wine. A classic from Burgundy, these are the perfect snack with Oregon Pinot noir. They are essentially savory cream puffs.

Makes about 40 puffs

1 cup water
1/2 cup unsalted butter
1 teaspoon salt
1 cup flour
5 whole large eggs
1 1/2 cups (5 ounces) grated Gruyère cheese
3 to 4 tablespoons grated Parmesan cheese

Special tools:
2 cookie sheets
Silpat or parchment paper
Pastry bag with star tip

Preheat the oven to 425°F.

Line 2 cookies sheets with silpat or parchment. Combine the water, butter, and salt into the saucepan. Bring to a boil, and make sure that the butter is completely melted. Add the flour, all at once, and stir vigorously with a wooden spoon. Remove from the heat. Blend well. The dough will form into a large ball. Continue to stir in the pan for a minute or two. This will dry the dough out slightly. Place the dough in the bowl of an electric mixer, fitted with a whip, and whip on medium speed for 2 to 3 minutes to cool the dough.

Continuing at medium to medium-high speed, add 4 of the eggs, one at a time, making sure each egg is well combined before adding the next. When the last egg is blended, add the grated Gruyère and blend thoroughly.

Remove the dough to a large pastry bag filled with a medium star tip. Pipe small mounds of the dough on the lined baking sheets, leaving at least 1 inch between each mound. The mounds should be about the diameter of a quarter and about 1-inch high.

Scramble the remaining egg, and brush the dough lightly with it. Sprinkle with the grated Parmesan. Bake for 10 minutes, reduce the oven heat to 350°F and bake about an additional 20 minutes. The dough should puff about double in size and be nicely browned.

Remove the puffs, poke a small hole or slit in the side of each to let the air escape or the puffs might deflate slightly. Serve immediately.

oeufs en meurette
poached eggs in pinot noir sauce

from Domaine Drouhin

This classic French recipe comes from fourth-generation winemaker Véronique Drouhin-Boss of Domaine Drouhin Oregon and Maison Joseph Drouhin of Burgundy. The founding of Domaine Drouhin Oregon in 1987, in the heart of the Dundee Hills, is considered a landmark event for the Oregon wine industry.

Serves 4

4 large eggs
1/2 cup chopped white mushrooms
2 tablespoons butter, divided
1/2 cup chopped bacon
1 onion, chopped
1 tablespoon flour
2 1/2 cups Domaine Drouhin Pinot Noir
1 bouquet garni
1 clove garlic, chopped
1 teaspoon sugar
Salt
Freshly ground black pepper
Bread slices, for grilled croutons
1 clove garlic, for rubbing on the bread

Sauté the mushrooms in 1 tablespoon of butter in a pan until slightly browned. In a separate pan, sauté the bacon with the onion and 1 tablespoon of butter. Add the flour to thicken the mixture to create a roux.

Add the wine, the bouquet garni, the mushrooms, garlic, and sugar. Salt and pepper to taste. Simmer on very low heat for approximately 45 minutes until the sauce thickens.

Sauté the bread slices in butter and rub the clove of garlic lightly over them. Just before serving, poach the eggs in the wine sauce.

avocado blini
with dungeness crab

from Chef William King

This is a beautiful appetizer or light lunch showcasing the interplay between hot and cold ingredients. I love it for freshness and color, and for the wonderful little pancakes made from fresh avocado that are its foundation.

Serves 4

For the blini batter:
1 medium avocado, puréed (Save about 2 tablespoons for the sauce.)
3/4 cup all-purpose flour
5 to 6 tablespoons milk
1/4 teaspoon salt
1 tablespoon freshly chopped chives
2 large eggs

Combine all of the ingredients, and blend well to form a medium-thick pancake batter. Cover, and reserve while you prepare the other elements.

For the avocado aïoli:
2 tablespoons avocado purée
4 tablespoons mayonnaise
2 tablespoons heavy cream
Pinch salt

Combine and blend thoroughly.

To assemble:
12 ounces Dungeness crab meat and legs
1 tablespoon oil
2 tablespoons butter
Blini batter
3/4 cup finely diced melon (Mango, papaya, red pepper—whatever you like to create a colorful "salsa.")
1 1/2 tablespoon freshly chopped chives
4 tablespoons avocado aïoli

Gather all of the ingredients. Heat 1 tablespoon of oil with 2 tablespoons of butter in a sauté pan. When the butter stops sizzling, add the blini batter in heaping tablespoons to form 2-inch pancakes. When the blini have lightly browned on one side, flip and continue to cook for 1 to 2 minutes.

Plate 3 blini for each serving and arrange the crab meat over them. Scatter the plate with the diced fruit and chopped chives. Drizzle with the avocado aïoli, and serve immediately while the blini are still warm.

WINE PAIRING
Archery Summit
1998 or 2001 Red Hills
Estate Pinot Noir

roasted fingerlings
with basil pesto and smoked trout

from Archery Summit

This is a hearty appetizer, or even a lunch item from Archery Summit. The potatoes are a great vehicle to bring the smoky flavor of the trout and the rich, herbaceous pesto together.

Serves 4 to 6 as an appetizer
Serves 2 as an entrée

2 hot-smoked trout fillets, skinned, deboned

Basil pesto:
2 bunches basil, leaves only
1/4 cup pine nuts, toasted
1/4 cup grated Parmesan cheese
6 cloves garlic, roasted
3/4 cup extra virgin olive oil
Salt
Freshly ground black pepper

Place the basil, pine nuts, Parmesan, and garlic in a food processor and pulse, while drizzling in the olive oil to form a rough paste. Season to taste with salt and pepper. Cover with plastic wrap and refrigerate to allow the flavors to mingle while preparing the potatoes.

Potatoes:
2 pounds fingerling potatoes, cut on the bias
2 tablespoons extra virgin olive oil
Salt
Freshly ground black pepper

Preheat the oven to 400°F.

Toss the cut potatoes with the olive oil and season with salt and pepper. Roast on a foil-lined sheet tray for 35 to 45 minutes, or until perfectly roasted and tender. Remove from the oven and let cool slightly. Toss with the basil pesto.

Place the smoked trout fillets in the oven to just warm. Place the fingerlings in a serving bowl. Shred the warm trout over the potatoes and serve warm.

parmesan tuille cups
or coronets

from Chef William King

These tuilles are a little touchy, but once you get the hang of it, they're simple and the work can go fast. These cheesy treats are worth the effort, and are a great item to use as hors d'oeuvres, or even as a garnish for salads. The only ingredient is freshly grated Parmesan cheese. Take a chunk of the cheese and run it across the medium-fine holes of a box grater just prior to assembling.

Makes about 24 cups or cornets

1 1/2 cups freshly grated Parmesan cheese

Special tools:
2 cookie sheets
Silpat
Small, flexible metal spatula

For the goat cheese-mascarpone mousse:
4 ounces fresh goat cheese
4 ounces mascarpone
1 tablespoon chopped chives
Pinch kosher salt
Freshly ground black pepper

Blend all ingredients thoroughly and puff or spoon into Parmesan cups or cornets.

To assemble: Preheat the oven to 350°F.

Line 2 cookie sheets with silpat. (You cannot do this directly on the pan and parchment paper is a poor substitute for this technique.) You can also use a nonstick pan, and it will work just as well. Place a 2 1/2-inch ring mold in one corner of the silpat and fill with a heaping tablespoon of the grated cheese, spreading it evenly over the inside surface of the ring. Remove the ring and repeat the process, about 1 1/2-inches away from the first circle, as the cheese will spread slightly when it melts. Continue the process until you have 8 circles of cheese on the silpat. Depending on how you want to shape the tuilles, have your molds ready (see below). Do only one thing at a time, as it is difficult to manage more than 8 of these tuilles as they come out of the oven.

Place the first tray in the oven. While the tuilles are baking, you can prepare the second tray, but don't put it in the oven yet. Bake the first tray of tuilles for about 8 to 9 minutes. They will be bubbly and lightly browned. Be careful not to oven-brown the tuilles, as they will become too brittle to mold as they cool. If you underbake them, they will not hold their shape. (Be prepared to ruin a tray or two while you practice.) Know you must move quickly as the tuilles only need to cool slightly, for no more than 10 to 15 seconds, so they hold their shape. They will quickly become too stiff and brittle to take a shape.

Remove each tuille, one by one, and shape on, in, or around your mold. You will find the tuilles malleable and forgiving, but only for a minute or two. If they get too stiff before you are done, put the tray back in the oven for 20 seconds. Repeat the process with the other trays. Once the tuilles are shaped they hold for several hours. Fill with your favorite mixture. Mine is goat-cheese mascarpone mousse.

Chef's note: for cups, use small muffin tins or even an egg carton. For cornets, you will need special, cone-shaped molds available at specialty cookware stores or baking and candy supply stores.

chicken hazelnut sausage
with roasted garlic and red pepper cream sauce

from Chef William King

This is a very nice starter for a formal meal but could also work as a lunch item. Using this simple technique creates a sausage, without the casing, that can be served several ways: sliced on crostini as an hors d'oeuvre (without the sauce), heated and sliced, or even sliced when cold, then sautéed in a little butter.

Makes 2 to 8 "sausages"

For the sausage:
2 tablespoons butter
3 tablespoons sherry
3/4 cup finely diced yellow onion
1 pound ground chicken (white, dark, or a mix)
1/2 pound ground pork (or mild bulk Italian or country sausage)
1/2 cup heavy cream
1 large egg
1/2 tablespoon minced garlic
1/8 teaspoon dried thyme
1 teaspoon salt
1 teaspoon freshly ground black pepper
3 ounces (about 1/2 cup) hazelnuts, toasted, skins removed, very coarsely chopped
Chicken stock, for cooking the sausage

Melt the butter and sherry in a sauté pan and add the onions. Cook until very soft but do not brown. Allow to cool.

When the onions have cooled, combine the remainder of the ingredients for the sausage, except the chicken stock, and blend well, either by hand with a wooden spoon, or in an electric mixer on medium-low speed using the paddle attachment. After the mixture is thoroughly blended, add it to the bowl of a food processor and process for about 30 to 45 seconds. The mixture should be fairly smooth but not too mushy. If you have a large processor, this can be done in one step. If a smaller machine is used, do it in 2 to 3 batches.

Set up a work surface so that you can lay about 16 inches of plastic out horizontally in front of you. Take half of the chicken mixture and shape it into an 8-inch long by 1 3/4- to 2-inch thick "log" and place it in the center of the plastic wrap. Carefully roll the mixture up. It should be fairly firm and will handle well. Create a sausage shape encased in the plastic wrap with about 4 inches of extra wrap on either end. Roll it tight by twisting the ends of the plastic. The "sausage" will form naturally as the ends twist tighter. Roll the sausage around a bit to get the shape right and to remove any air bubbles. Repeat this process with the remainder of the mixture to form a second sausage.

Meanwhile, place a large sauté pan on the stove with chicken stock and/or water in it, and add a splash of sherry. Bring it to a boil, then reduce to a simmer. Add the two sausage rolls, cover, and simmer for 4 to 5 minutes. The liquid should rise halfway up the sides of the rolls. Rotate the sausage rolls so that all sides cook evenly and simmer for another 7 to 9 minutes. During the process the plastic may fall away from the sausage, this is not a problem as the mixture will have set and will remain firm. The stock will enhance the flavor with the wrap removed.

Carefully remove the sausage rolls to a plate to drain and cool slightly. You can check the internal temperature of the rolls; they should reach 140°F. Cool and slice, or slice and serve immediately with the Roasted Garlic Red Pepper Cream Sauce.

For the roasted garlic red pepper cream sauce:
1 cup chicken stock or broth
10 large cloves of garlic, oven roasted until soft and lightly brown
3 cups heavy cream
3 tablespoons roasted, finely diced peppers
Salt
Freshly ground black pepper
Freshly chopped chives or parsley, for garnish

Combine all of the ingredients and simmer to reduce the liquid to 2 cups. Carefully purée the mixture in a blender or food processor. Pool the sauce on a serving plate and arrange the sliced sausage over it. Scatter chopped chives or parsley on top to garnish.

antipasto of shrimp
with summer herbs

from Ponzi Vineyards

We love colorful, fragrant platters of antipasti all year long, but in summer it's especially tempting to ignore the "anti" part and just call it dinner. After all, one of the current restaurant trends is offering exciting, unusual, at times wildly contrasting flavor combinations under menu headings such as "small plates," "first dishes," "starters," "tapas"…antipasti. The shrimp in this recipe may be less exotic but they're readily available at your market and will create an equally delicious, little-bit-sweet, little-bit-salty, very pretty antipasti.

Serves 6 to 8

2 pounds large (16 to 20 count) shrimp
28 ounces cooking liquid (water and/or white wine—this is a
  great place to use leftover wine, especially something with a
  little sweetness like the last bit of vino gelato.)
1 tablespoon coarse salt
1 tablespoon curry powder
1 tablespoon peeled, chopped ginger
1 small clove garlic, chopped
1 cup roughly chopped summer herbs: Italian parsley, chervil,
  thyme, tarragon, and basil
Good quality olive oil, for garnish
Balsamic vinegar, for garnish
Medium/coarse salt, for garnish

Bring the liquid, salt, curry powder, ginger, and garlic to a boil. Add the herbs and shrimp. Cover and return to a boil, approximately 5 minutes. Take care not to overcook.

Immediately place the shrimp in bowl of cold water to stop the cooking process. Clean, cover well with plastic wrap, and reserve in the refrigerator.

Accompany the shrimp with a small bowl of dipping sauce made by blending the olive oil, balsamic vinegar, and salt. Alternatively and with a tiny bit more effort, you can make a light mayonnaise in the food processor using the same ingredients, a very fresh egg, and a little lemon juice.

chef's tips for preparing shrimp

- Run cold water over the shrimp for 2 minutes before cooking to avoid toughness.
- Shrimp cook quickly and are ruined by overcooking. Rule of thumb: Medium: 3 to 4 minutes; large: 5 to 7 minutes; jumbo: 7 to 8 minutes.
- Always cool immediately.
- Shrimp must be shelled and deveined. (Run the tip of a sharp knife down the back of the shrimp to remove the vein.)
- Some people find that cleaning the shrimp before cooking is easier. If you clean them first, reduce the cooking time slightly.

spring onion sformato

from Nick's Italian Café

Nick's Italian Café in the heart of the Willamette Valley has been a gathering place for many of the area winemakers since it opened in 1977. This Italian custard from Chef Carmen Peirano is a richly flavored savory pudding that resembles a fallen soufflé. The name comes from the Italian for "unmolded." Don't worry that it rises and then falls—it's just the nature of the dish.

Serves 10

Unsalted butter, softened, for preparing the tartlet tins
2 pounds spring onions
2 tablespoons butter
2 tablespoons all-purpose flour
3 cups milk
1/4 cup grated Parmesan cheese
Salt
10 whole eggs
1 tablespoon champagne vinegar

Preheat the oven to 325°F.

Grease the tartlet tins or ramekins generously with the softened butter. Cut the spring onions into a julienne and slowly sweat over medium heat until the onions are tender and translucent.

While the onions are slowly cooking down, prepare a béchamel. Melt the butter in a saucepan, and add the flour until the mixture is the consistency of wet sand. Let this cook for two minutes, making sure that you do not brown the mixture. Slowly add the milk, whisking continuously, until the mixture comes to a boil. Set aside.

After the onions have cooked down, transfer them to a blender and purée until smooth. Mix the warm purée, Parmesan and the béchamel. Season to taste.

Break the eggs into a large mixing bowl and beat them. Add the champagne vinegar. Slowly add the onion mixture into the beaten eggs stirring constantly, and taste for seasoning. Fill the buttered tartlet tins with the mixture. Place the tartlet tins in a baking dish and carefully add water until reaches about 1/3 of the way up the sides of the tartlet tins.

Bake until set, let cool slightly and turn out of the molds onto a serving platter or individual dishes. Garnish with fried parsley leaves, a fresh salad or a simple drizzle of extra virgin olive oil.

WINE PAIRING
Bethel Heights Vineyard
2007 Oregon Pinot Gris

oregon style pâté

from Bethel Heights Vineyard

This pâté, rich with the chicken livers, yet a bit sweet from currants and spices, pairs well with both Pinot noir and pinot gris. An off-dry pinot gris offers a refreshing citrus contrast to the pâté, while still having enough sweetness and body to balance the chicken and currants. That said, the pâté is equally at home with a young, fruit-driven Pinot noir, complementing the texture and meaty richness of the livers.

Serves 4 to 6

1/2 cup dried currants
1/4 cup dry or off-dry white wine
1/4 cup cognac
1/2 large onion, minced
1 tablespoon unsalted butter
1 pound whole chicken livers, preferably from free-range, hormone-free chickens
1 clove garlic, peeled, crushed

1/8 teaspoon ground allspice
1/8 teaspoon nutmeg or mace
1/8 teaspoon freshly ground black pepper
1/4 teaspoon salt
1 (8-ounce) package Neufchâtel (light cream cheese), softened to room temperature
1 tablespoon freshly minced parsley
1 tablespoon freshly minced chives

Soak the currants in the wine and cognac, and reserve. Allow them to soak for 4 to 5 hours.

Sauté the onions over medium heat in butter until they are translucent, about 5 to 8 minutes. Add the chicken livers and garlic. Turn the livers often, so they cook evenly but are still barely pink inside when cut, about 10 minutes. Transfer the liver mixture to a food processor fitted with a blade. Add the spices and blend in the cream cheese, cut into small chunks, and add gradually until the mixture is smooth and creamy. Place the mixture in a mixing bowl.

Drain the currants from the wine and cognac, reserving the liquid for another use. By hand, stir in the currants, parsley, and chives. Chill until ready to serve, removing from the refrigerator 15 minutes before serving.

WINE PAIRING
Sokol Blosser Winery
2005 Estate Cuvée
Pinot Noir

smoked duck on corn cakes

from Chef William King

Smoked duck breast is one of my favorite foods. Rich, smoky, a nice band of fat surrounding rosy, pink meat… and you can purchase it if you don't have the time or inclination to smoke it yourself. I do, and it makes for a very convenient foundation for appetizers and salads. In this recipe it creates great balance of cold against the hot, crispy corn cakes, and richness against their slightly spicy sweetness.

Serves 4 as an appetizer

For the corn cakes:

2 1/2 cups corn kernels, fresh from the cob (1/2 puréed, 1/2 whole)
1/2 cup milk
2 eggs
4 egg yolks
1/2 teaspoon baking powder

1/2 cup all-purpose flour
1/2 cup cornmeal
Pinch cayenne pepper
1/2 teaspoon salt
Pinch freshly ground black pepper
Vegetable oil, for frying

Combine all the ingredients, except the oil, to form a fairly thick batter.

For the maple aïoli:

8 tablespoons mayonnaise
1 egg yolk
2 tablespoons maple syrup
1 tablespoon cider vinegar

Combine all of the ingredients, and reserve.

To assemble:

Smoked duck breast, sliced thinly into 12 slices
Very finely julienned sweet red pepper, for garnish
Micro greens, for garnish (or spicy radish sprouts)

Heat the oil, about 3 to 4 tablespoons at a time in a non-stick sauté pan. Give the corn cake batter a quick stir, and add it in tablespoon-sized dollops to the pan. Press lightly on the tops of the batter dollops with the spoon to form 1 1/2 to 2-inch "pancakes." Allow them to brown for about 1 minute, then flip and brown on the second side for a minute or so.

Remove the corn cakes to drain briefly on paper towels. Add more oil if necessary, and continue to make them until you have 12 to 16.

Place 3 to 4 cakes on each serving plate, and top with the smoked duck slices. Garnish the duck with the red pepper strips and micro greens. Drizzle the maple aïoli over all, and serve immediately.

WINE PAIRING
EdenVale Winery
Viognier, Grenache *or*
MidSummer's Eve

spicy oregon pear salsa
with oregon jack cheese and hazelnut crisps

from EdenVale Winery

Here's a very Oregonian, quick, fun and tasty snack or party item. The pear salsa is also delicious on grilled chicken or pork.

Serves 4 to 6

Spicy Oregon Pear Salsa:
2 large firm Oregon pears
3 tablespoons freshly squeezed lemon juice
2 tablespoons sugar
1/2 to 1 small jalapeño pepper, seeded, finely chopped
1/2 teaspoon salt
1/2 cup finely chopped red onion

Cheese And Hazelnut Crisps:
6 small (8-inch) tortillas
2 cups shredded Oregon Jack cheese
3/4 cup coarsely chopped, raw Oregon hazelnuts

Preheat oven to 400°F.

Cut the pears in half and core. Cut into small (1/4-inch) dice. Mix the pears, lemon juice, sugar, pepper, salt and onion. Cover, and refrigerate. Store up to three days.

Lay the tortillas on foil or parchment-lined baking sheets and sprinkle with cheese and hazelnuts. With a large knife or pizza cutter, cut each tortilla into 8 wedges. Bake for 7 to 10 minutes, or until the cheese is bubbling and the tortillas are browned and crisp. Serve immediately topped with the salsa.

Chef's note: This recipe works best with firm pears found at the grocery stores. Pears ripened for eating will be too soft.

"Good wine is a good creature if it is well used."

—WILLIAM SHAKESPEARE

WINE PAIRING
Ponzi Vineyards
2006 Arneis

sea scallop "ratatouille"

from The Dundee Bistro

Dundee Bistro Chef Jason Stoller Smith creates a fresh and colorful "ratatouille" accompaniment to richly flavored East Coast sea scallops.

Serves 2

2 ounces (U/10 count) dry pack sea scallops
1 cucumber, sliced very thin into circles on a mandolin
1 yellow squash, sliced very thin into circles on a mandolin
2 ounces grape tomatoes, sliced very thin on a mandolin
1 tablespoon champagne vinegar
1 tablespoon niçoise olives, pitted, julienned
1 shallot, minced
1/2 tablespoon fresh thyme leaves
3 tablespoons extra virgin olive oil
Kosher salt
Freshly ground black pepper
4 sprigs Italian flat leafed parsley, stemmed, chiffonade
1 lemon, julienned zest

Arrange the cucumbers in a layered circle on the plate. Arrange the slices of yellow squash just inside the ring of cucumbers, followed by the tomatoes. You should have 3 distinct rings of the 3 vegetables.

Mix together the vinegar, olives, shallot and thyme in a bowl. Slowly whisk in the olive oil and correct the seasoning with salt and pepper. Drizzle on top of the salad rings.

Toss the scallops in the reserve dressing. Sear the scallops in a hot pan with a dash of olive oil until done. A sea scallop is perfectly done when medium to medium-rare.

Arrange the scallops in middle of the plate. Combine the parsley and lemon zest, and scatter the mixture over the scallops.

Chef's note: "Dry pack" refers to the limited processing that the best scallops receive and is a strong indication of good quality.

marinated sardines

from Nick's Italian Café

If you've never had fresh sardines, this recipe provides an opportunity to try the wonderful little fish. Forget the tin cans with the twist keys. This presentation from Chef Carmen Peirano, a "crudo" that relies on lemon, salt, thyme, and good olive oil, is freshness at its best.

Serves 8

16 fresh sardines, filleted
3 tablespoons sea salt
1 bunch fresh thyme
Juice of 2 lemons, strained
4 tablespoons extra virgin olive oil, plus extra for garnish

Place the fillets of sardine, flesh-side-down, in a shallow dish. Sprinkle them with salt and top with thyme sprigs. Pour the lemon juice and olive oil over the fillets. Marinate, refrigerated for 1 hour.

Remove the sardines from the marinade, place on a platter or individual plates, drizzle with olive oil, and serve.

---

a couple of "big hitters"

Oregon is not known for its large wineries sprawling hundreds of acres. To the contrary, some of our winemakers produce less than 200 barrels a year. That is why, even though there are more than 300 wineries in the state, we still trail California and Washington by wide margins when it comes to wine production. We do have wine growers whose acreage and production are very impressive. Jim Bernau founded Willamette Valley Vineyards in 1983 and has since expanded to several sites that sit majestically above the I-5 corridor in the middle of the Willamette Valley. The crowning jewel of the property is the world-class winery where the winemakers perform their magic. Jim is a leader in several ways. His strict standards of viticulture have earned his sites LIVE certification, and the Salmon Safe Seal, as well as being certified sustainable. On the business side of things, Willamette Valley Vineyards is unusual in that Jim has sold shares of vineyard ownership to the public, and now boasts over 4,500 owners!

The other "big" success story is King Estates. Established by Ed King III and his family in the early nineties, King Estates now cultivates vineyards on over 1,000 acres in the southern Willamette Valley region. Their magnificent estate is home to its 110,000 square foot winery, as well as beautiful orchards and lush gardens. It continues as a family-owned business today. Yet, King Estates prides itself for its "collective effort" in its wine-making approach. Wine maker Bill Kramer is joined by a team including John Albran and Lindsay Kamff, to produce the state's largest volume of wine. Yet, even considering its size, King Estates' approach to viticulture is consistent with Oregon's overall philosophic commitment to sustainable-farming practices. Congratulations to both of these wine powers who have proven that "bigger" and "better" are not mutually exclusive terms.

edenvale winery's sangria

from EdenVale Winery

Wine "snobs" often turn up their noses at the thought of blending wines and fruits. Let there be more sangria for you and me to enjoy on a hot evening when the occasion is casual and the food fits the bill! Refreshing and very durable, sangria and light, rosé-style wine have been staples of summertime meals throughout the Mediterranean and in Latin countries around the world. It is also an answer to what to eat with highly spiced foods as the chill and sweetness of a good sangria are ideal counterpoints to the "heat" on the palate.

1 orange
1 lemon
1 lime
1 red apple
1 peach
1 part EdenVale Heritage Red Wine
1 part EdenVale Midsummer's Eve
16 ounces club soda
Crushed ice

Cut the fruit into small wedges. Mix together the red wine, white wine, and club soda. Add the fruit, and fill the rest of the pitcher with crushed ice. Chill for at least 2 hours before serving.

"A man will be eloquent if you give him good wine."

—RALPH WALDO EMERSON, *Representative Men*

soups & salads

From a rich lamb stew to a delicate crab salad, this eclectic section is as varied as the chefs whose recipes appear here.

WINE PAIRING
Wooldridge Creek
Syrah

french lentil, barley & chicken soup
with goat cheese crostini

from Wooldridge Creek Vineyard and Winery

Each year as fall turns to winter, this soup feeds Kara Olmo's family. It is fragrant, satisfying and smells so inviting that you just might have neighbors stopping by to investigate. French lentils supply wonderful flavor—a little herbal—a little spicy, as well as giving the soup great texture. Pair it with a Wooldridge Creek Syrah, made in the style of a Northern Rhone wine.

Serves 6

2 cups cooked, shredded chicken
2 teaspoons olive oil
3 ounces chopped pancetta
3 ribs celery, diced
2 carrots, diced
1 medium onion, diced
5 cloves garlic, chopped
3 tablespoons tomato paste
1 cup red wine
6 cups low-sodium beef stock
2 tablespoons dried Italian seasonings
4 tablespoons freshly chopped oregano
Salt
Freshly ground black pepper
1 cup dry, small green lentils, rinsed
1 cup medium pearl barley

Goat cheese crostini:
1 baguette, sliced
3 ounces goat cheese
Freshly ground black pepper

To prepare the soup, heat a large soup pot over medium-high heat. Add the olive oil, pancetta, celery, carrots and onion. Sauté for 5 minutes. Add the garlic, and sauté for 1 minute. Add the tomato paste and stir until well combined. Stir in the wine and the stock. Add the dried and fresh herbs, salt, and pepper. Add the lentils and barley, and bring to a boil.

Reduce the heat to medium-low, and add the chicken. Cover, and simmer until the barley and lentils are tender, stirring occasionally, about 1 hour. If the soup is too thick, add a little water.

Preheat the oven to 400°F.

Toast the baguette slices until they are very lightly toasted. Remove from the oven and top each slice with a little crumbled goat cheese. Return to the oven just until the cheese melts. Top with freshly ground black pepper. Serve the crostini alongside the soup.

WINE PAIRING
Spangler Vineyards
2006 Syrah

duck-sausage gumbo

from Spangler Vineyards

Cajun comes to Oregon! Duck is rich and flavorful, and adds depth to this spicy stew from Chef Scott Rutter. The secret is the charring of the duck that creates a smoky round flavor and adds a nice dark, rich color to the finished product. Filé powder, also called gumbo filé, is a spice made from dried and ground sassafras leaves. When sprinkled sparingly over gumbo as a seasoning, it adds a distinctive flavor and texture.

Serves 6 to 8

1 (3 to 5-pound) domestic duck, quartered
4 tablespoons Cajun seasoning
2 tablespoons olive oil
8 ounces diced smoked German sausage
1 1/2 cups diced yellow onion
1 cup diced green pepper
1 cup diced celery
1 tablespoon filé powder
Salt
Freshly ground black pepper

Preheat the charcoal or gas grill to medium high.

Liberally dust the duck with half of the Cajun seasoning. Grill to lightly char the duck on all sides. Remove from heat and allow to cool.

Heat a 4-quart Dutch oven on the stove over medium heat. Add the olive oil and diced sausage. Lightly brown the sausage. Add the onion, green pepper, celery, and the remainder of the Cajun seasoning. Cook the vegetables until tender, add the duck, and cover with water. Reduce the heat to simmer and cover the pot.

Cook the duck for approximately 2 hours. Cool and remove the duck quarters from gumbo, and debone. Skim the fat from the top of the gumbo. Return the duck meat to the gumbo, and add the filé powder. Season to taste with salt and pepper. Reheat and serve.

belgian endive salad
with king estate pears, blue cheese, and orange champagne vinaigrette

from King Estate Winery

A classic blend of bitter, sweet, tart and rich, this salad is a delicious addition to a meal that might feature grilled or roasted meats as its main course. Chef Michael Landsberg pairs the tender crunch of endive leaves with juicy pears fresh from the garden in this winter salad.

Serves 4

2 medium to ripe pears (Asian, Bosc, Anjou, Seckel, Bartlett)
4 large Belgian endive leaves, cored
1/2 cup Rogue Creamery Oregon Blue cheese
2 tablespoons chopped herbs (Any combination of parsley, chives, tarragon, chervil, or thyme.)
Salt
Freshly ground black pepper

For the orange champagne vinaigrette :
4 navel oranges, juiced
3 tablespoons champagne vinegar
2/3 cup extra virgin olive oil
Salt
Freshly ground black pepper

To prepare the vinaigrette, reduce the juice of the four oranges by half, until the liquid is slightly syrupy. Allow the reduction to cool. Combine the orange juice with the champagne vinegar, olive oil, and salt and pepper.

Core the pears, and slice them into wedges. In a salad bowl, add the endive leaves and crumble the blue cheese over the top. Add the pears and the chopped herbs. Season to taste with salt and pepper. Toss the salad with the vinaigrette, and enjoy.

about king estate winery

The marriage of food and wine has been central to King Estate Winery's practice of viticulture from its inception in 1991. Besides growing grapes and making wine, King Estate cultivates forty-five acres of organic gardens and orchards. Most of the fresh fruit, vegetables, and herbs used in their culinary program and featured in their restaurant are grown on site.

WINE PAIRING
Cowhorn Vineyard
Viognier

golden beet salad
hazelnut-crusted goat cheese

from Chateaulin Restaurant Français

There are many rich, complex flavors and fresh ingredients utilized in this beautiful salad. But, sometimes that's what it takes to create something very special. The ring mold presentation is a professional touch from Chef David Taub. If you don't have one, don't worry, presenting it "free-style" is perfectly fine.

Serves 4

Prepare a day in advance:

Chive oil:
2 cups chives
2 cups grapeseed oil

Blanch the chives briefly in a pot of boiling, salted water. Immediately shock them in cold water, and drain thoroughly. Squeeze out any excess water, and place in a blender with the oil. Purée for 3 to 4 minutes. Pour into a container and refrigerate for 24 hours. Strain through a fine sieve before using.

Marinated Montrachet:
4 (2-ounce) portions Montrachet goat cheese
Extra virgin olive oil

Marinate the goat cheese in enough oil to cover. Let soak for 24 hours.

Prepare a few hours before serving:

Red beet essence:
1 pound red beets, peeled, coarsely chopped
1 tablespoon arrowroot powder

In a small saucepot, add just enough water to cover the beets and bring to a low boil. Cook over medium heat until fork tender. Puree the beets and water with an immersion blender. Continue to cook until reduced by half. Strain through a fine sieve, and return to the saucepot. Blend the arrowroot with 1 tablespoon cold water, and add to the warm beet purée. Bring to a boil, and strain again into a container. Reserve.

Continued on the next page...

golden beet salad *continued...*

Vinaigrette:
1 teaspoon Dijon mustard
1 teaspoon honey
1 ounce white balsamic vinegar
3 ounces olive oil
Salt, to taste
Freshly ground black pepper, to taste

Whisk together the Dijon mustard, honey, and vinegar in a small bowl. Whisk in the oil slowly until incorporated. Season to taste with salt and pepper. Reserve.

Roasted golden beets:
3 medium golden beets, washed, rubbed with olive oil

Preheat the oven to 350°F.

Roast the beets for about 1 1/2 hours until a paring knife goes through them without resistance. Chill completely, then peel and cut into julienne.

To assemble:
1 Belgian endive, julienne
1/2 cup radicchio, julienne
1 small head frisée, washed, chopped
Vinaigrette
Roasted golden beets
1/4 medium red onion, julienne
1 tablespoon lightly chopped fresh dill
1 tablespoon lightly chopped fresh chives
1 1/2 tablespoons olive oil
1/2 tablespoon champagne vinegar
Salt
Freshly ground black pepper
Marinated Montrachet goat cheese
1 cup toasted, chopped hazelnuts
Red beet essence, for garnish
Chive oil, for garnish

Preheat the oven to 400°F.

Toss the endive, radicchio, and frisée with the vinaigrette. Set aside.

Toss the roasted beets with the red onion, dill, chives, olive oil, and vinegar. Season to taste with salt and pepper to taste. Set aside.

Drain the cheese, and coat completely with the chopped hazelnuts. Bake for about 5 to 6 minutes, until warmed through but not runny.

Meanwhile, use a ring mold, place 1/4 of the endive mixture on a plate, and top with 1/4 of the beet mixture. Repeat onto three more plates. Top each with a piece of goat cheese, and garnish with pools of red beet essence and chive oil. Serve immediately.

pea and crab salad

from Cristom Vineyards

The fresh crab and English peas make this a fantastic lunch salad that pairs well with Cristom's Estate Viognier or Estate Pinot Gris, both of which have enough ripeness and body to balance the richness of the crab meat. This seasonal salad is wonderful throughout the late spring and early summer. It is a Cristom family favorite inspired by Mark Bittman's New York Times column, "The Minimalist."

Serves 4 or more

6 to 8 ounces freshly cooked Dungeness crabmeat
1 1/2 cups shelled fresh English peas (or frozen)
1 medium white onion, finely chopped
1/2 red or yellow bell pepper (or a combination), minced
3 tablespoons extra virgin olive oil
Freshly squeezed lemon juice
Salt
Freshly ground black pepper
4 iceberg lettuce leaves or 16 endive leaves, washed, dried
Freshly shredded basil leaves, for garnish (or chopped parsley)

Bring a small pot of salted water to a boil. Poach the peas until they are bright green, about 30 seconds. Remove the peas with a slotted spoon, and drop into iced water to chill. Drain.

In a large mixing bowl, combine the peas, onion, bell pepper, crab, olive oil, and lemon juice. Season to taste with salt and pepper, and add more lemon juice and/or olive oil, if necessary.

To serve, spoon the salad into lettuce cups or on top of the endive leaves. Garnish with the basil, and serve.

"One barrel of wine can work more miracles than a church full of saints."

—ITALIAN PROVERB

beef & veal

Oregon has become as dedicated to sustainable animal husbandry practices as it is to quality wine production. This section offers recipes utilizing cuts of meat from several of our region's finest beef producers.

WINE PAIRING
Willakenzie Estate
2006 Willamette Valley
Pinot Noir

fricasse of veal
"facon grandmere"

from Willakenzie Estate Winery

*This classic veal fricassee comes from Chef Paul Bachand's grandmother, and was a family favorite
from his childhood. It is at its best when made in the springtime when the morels, English peas, and
Jerusalem artichokes are in season. This is a Sunday supper par excellence!*

Serves 4

2 pounds veal shoulder, cut into 2-inch pieces
Kosher salt
Freshly ground white pepper
1 1/2 cups unsalted butter
1 1/2 cups finely chopped celery
1 1/2 cups finely chopped leek
1/2 cup flour
2 cups dry white wine
4 cups blonde veal stock or beef broth
4 cups whole milk
1 pound preferably fresh (or dried) morels
8 ciopollini onions or small boiler onions
6 sunchokes (Jerusalem artichokes)
1 cup fresh English peas
1 tablespoon freshly chopped thyme
1 tablespoon freshly chopped parsley
1 tablespoon freshly chopped chervil

Preheat the oven to 325°F.

Season the veal with salt and white pepper, and reserve. Melt the butter in a deep sauté pan or rondeau. Add the meat and "sweat" over very low heat until it is no longer pink on the outside. (Do not brown the meat. This is a blonde sauce, so you do not want any color on the meat.) Transfer the veal to a bowl and reserve.

Cook the leeks and celery over low heat until soft. Add the flour, and cook for 3 minutes over low heat. Add the white wine and reduce until almost dry. Return the meat to the pan along with the veal stock and milk. Bring to a slow boil, cover, and roast in the oven for 3 hours, or until tender.

Remove the meat carefully from the pan, strain the sauce into a large sauce pan, keeping the meat warm for service. Add the morels, onions, and sunchokes to the sauce and cook for an additional 20 minutes over medium heat until the sunchokes and onions are tender. Season to taste with salt and pepper. Dust with the chopped herbs, and serve.

boeuf d'oregon

from Scott Paul Wines

This is the Wright family's twist on the classic French dish, boeuf bourguignon. Since they make Oregon Pinot noir, and also import wines from fifteen small producers in Burgundy, this dish represents the sum of their passion for pinot, on both sides of the pond! The preparation could not be simpler, and the results are instant comfort for a hungry crew. (The secret is browning the meat over high heat in small batches. Then slow roasting for a long time.)

Serves 8 to 10

4 pounds boneless beef chuck roast, trimmed, cut into 1 1/4-inch cubes
Salt
Freshly ground black pepper
1/4 cup olive oil
3 large yellow onions, sliced to 1/4-inch thick
2 cups baby carrots
1 pound white mushrooms, sliced
1 tablespoon Worcestershire sauce
1 bottle Pinot noir (or more)
1/4 cup tomato paste

Season the meat generously with salt and pepper. Heat the olive oil in a Dutch oven over medium-high heat. Brown the meat on all sides, in batches. Remove the meat and reserve.

Add the onions and carrots to the pot and sauté, stirring frequently until they soften, adding a bit more oil if necessary. Add the mushrooms, cover the pot, and cook until softened, about an additional 5 minutes.

Remove and reserve the vegetables, and return the meat to the pot. Add the Worcestershire sauce and wine. Cover, and simmer over low heat for 1 hour. Add the tomato paste, and the reserved vegetables, and continue to cook, uncovered, for another 30 minutes, or until fork-tender. Check occasionally to see if more liquid is required. The finished consistency should be thickened so as to coat the meat and vegetables. Serve over rice, polenta, or buttered egg noodles.

"Wine makes daily living easier, less hurried, with fewer tensions and more tolerance."

—BENJAMIN FRANKLIN

WINE PAIRING
Spangler Vineyards
2006 Cabernet Franc

prosciutto-wrapped stuffed beef tenderloin

with goat cheese and basil mashed potatoes and shoestring carrots

from Spangler Vineyards

This is a lovely and unique way to add interest to a roasted or grilled beef tenderloin. Some might say this is "gilding the lily," but I say beef tenderloin needs added elements to give it spark, and this is it—crisped prosciutto wrapping, mushroom-herb butter filling and great accompaniments.

Serves 6 to 8

1 (4 to 5-pound) beef tenderloin, cleaned (All fat and silver skin removed.)
1 pound thinly sliced prosciutto

Stuffing:
1 teaspoon olive oil
2 tablespoons butter
1/4 pound each: crimini, shiitake and oyster mushrooms, cleaned, coarsely chopped
1 teaspoon fresh tarragon, stemmed, coarsely chopped
I teaspoon fresh thyme, stemmed, coarsely chopped
1/4 cup white wine

Goat cheese and basil mashed potatoes:
4 large russet potatoes, peeled, cubed
1/2 cup heavy cream
4 tablespoons butter
Salt
Freshly ground black pepper
8 ounces goat cheese
6 large basil leaves, finely chopped

Shoestring carrots:
3 large carrots, peeled, julienned
1 tablespoon butter
Salt
Freshly ground black pepper

To prepare the stuffing heat a sauté pan on medium heat, and add the olive oil and butter. Once the butter is melted, add the chopped mushrooms, and sauté until tender. Add the herbs, and deglaze with wine. Remove from the heat and allow to cool.

Butterfly the whole tenderloin lengthwise and prepare it for stuffing. Add the stuffing down the middle of the open tenderloin. Close the roll and wrap completely with the sliced prosciutto. Reserve.

Preheat the gas or charcoal grill to 350°F. This recipe works best when using an indirect cooking method.

To prepare the potatoes, place a large stock pot on the stove, on high heat with 3 quarts of water. Add the potatoes, and salt, and bring to a boil. Cook until the potatoes are fork-tender. Drain and mash using a hand potato masher, adding the cream, butter, salt and pepper until a smooth consistency is achieved. Stir in the goat cheese and basil, and cover to keep hot.

Placed the wrapped tenderloin on the barbecue for 25 minutes, or until an internal temperature of 120°F is reached. Remove and cover loosely with foil, allowing the tenderloin to rest for ten minutes before carving it into 1 1/2-inch pieces.

While the meat is resting, sauté the carrots in butter and salt and pepper until just tender. Serve with the potatoes and tenderloin.

short ribs
braised in oregon syrah

from Dobbes Family Estate

Joe Dobbes, owner, winemaker, and family chef was inspired to create this recipe from the great Chef Daniel Boulud's Café Boulud Cookbook. It is very deeply flavored and calls for an equally deep, spicy and flavorful wine. Joe suggests his Grand Assemblage Syrah. I do as well.

Serves 6 to 8

8 short ribs, trimmed of excess fat
3 bottles Oregon Syrah
2 tablespoons vegetable oil
Salt
Crushed black peppercorns
Flour, for dredging
8 large shallots, peeled, trimmed, split, rinsed, dried
2 medium-sized carrots, peeled, trimmed, cut into 1-inch lengths
2 ribs celery, peeled, trimmed, cut into 1-inch lengths
1 medium-sized leek (white and light-green parts), washed, dried, coarsely chopped
10 cloves garlic, peeled
6 sprigs flat-leaf parsley
2 bay leaves
2 thyme sprigs
2 tablespoons tomato paste
3 quarts unsalted beef broth
Freshly ground white pepper

Center a rack in the oven and preheat to 350°F.

Pour the wine into a large sauce pan and set over medium heat. (Make sure to pour some into a glass to drink.) When the wine is hot, carefully set it aflame. Let the flames die out, then increase the heat so that the wine boils. Allow the wine to boil until it cooks down by half. Remove from the heat.

Warm the oil in a large, heavy, ovenproof pot over medium-high heat. Season the ribs all over with salt and the crushed pepper. Dust half of the ribs with about 1 tablespoon of flour.

When the oil is hot, slip the ribs into the pot and sear for 4 to 5 minutes on each side, until well-browned. Transfer the ribs to a plate. Repeat with remaining ribs.

Remove all but 1 tablespoon of the fat from the pot, reduce the heat under the pot to medium and toss in the vegetables and herbs. Brown the vegetables lightly, about 5 to 7 minutes, then stir in the tomato paste and cook for 1 minute.

Add the wine, ribs, and broth to the pot. Bring to a boil, cover tightly, and place in the oven to braise for 2 1/2 hour, or until the ribs are very tender. Every 30 minutes, skim and discard the fat from the surface. (It's best to make the recipe to this point, cool, and chill the ribs and broth in the pan overnight, and scrape off the fat the next day. Rewarm before continuing.)

Carefully transfer the meat to a platter, and keep warm. Boil the pan liquid until it has reduced to 1 quart. Season with salt and white pepper. Pass through a fine strainer, and discard the solids. (The ribs and sauce can be combined and kept covered in the refrigerator for 2 to 3 days. Reheat gently, basting frequently, on top of the stove or in a 350°F oven.)

Serve one or two short ribs on prepared polenta and spoon the sauce liberally over the ribs. Enjoy with a big glass of Grande Assemblage Syrah!

cookie's stuffed steak

from Zerba Cellars

Dana Retz shares this story: "This is one of my mom, Carol Smith's recipes. She has been nicknamed "Cookie" because she is a great cook and loves to entertain. This recipe has become one of our favorites for entertaining guests on the back deck. These stuffed steaks are so flavorful that all you need to complement them is a crisp green salad, some fresh corn-on-the-cob, and a good red wine!"

Serves 4

4 (8-ounce) filet mignon steaks (about 1 1/2-inches thick)
3 tablespoons good-quality olive oil
2 fresh jalapeño peppers, seeded, diced
4 large cloves garlic, minced
4 (1 by 1/2-inch) wedges of white Cheddar cheese
4 wooden toothpicks
Salt
Freshly ground black pepper

Prepare the coals in a barbecue grill or preheat a gas grill.

Heat the olive oil in a small sauté pan, over medium heat. When the oil is hot, add the jalapeño peppers and sauté until they just start to become tender, for about 3 minutes. Add the minced garlic and stir. Cook until the garlic softens, for about 2 minutes, being careful not to let it burn. Remove from the heat and allow to cool slightly.

Prepare the steaks by cutting an opening in the side about 1 1/2 inches wide and 1 1/2 inches deep. With a teaspoon, scoop one spoonful of the pepper-garlic mixture into the opening in each steak. Slide in a wedge of Cheddar, pushing until the wedge is completely in. Close the opening with a toothpick. Season with salt and pepper.

Place the stuffed steaks on the hot grill, for 3 to 4 minutes on each side for medium doneness. Remove immediately from the grill to a serving platter. Cover with a loose tent of foil and allow to rest for 5 minutes.

---

beyond the valley

Oregon's Willamette Valley is the cornerstone of our wine industry. Rightly so, its terroir is producing the world's finest Pinot noir. It is home to our state's most highly regarded wineries and provides visitors with a concise centralized "path" to travel for their weekend tasting trips. In truth, it is the central focus of Oregon's restaurant industry and its agricultural bounty. But that is definitely not the whole story. Oregon enjoys seven official American Viticulture Areas (AVAs). To the north and east of the Willamette Valley are the Columbia Gorge and Walla Walla Valley districts, which border on the Columbia River and Washington State. To the south, the Umpqua, Rogue, and Applegate Valleys complete the group. Emerging wine growers, such as Viento in the Gorge, Zerba in the Walla Walla Valley area, Abacela, and Reustle-Prayer Rock down in the Umpqua, and RoxyAnn and Trium in the Rogue lead a developing group of wineries that respond to their growing environments with wines such as Merlot, Syrah, Viognier, Tempranillo, and Malbec. They may not be the "big hitters" that our Pinot noir and Pinot gris are, but these are quality winemakers producing quality wines. Stay tuned…Oregon's wine industry is just getting started!

WINE PAIRING
Scott Paul Wines
2006 Audrey Pinot Noir

easy osso buco

from Scott Paul Wines

I didn't believe it until I tried it, but the onions and tomatoes, simmered slowly with the meat, provide enough moisture to braise the veal shanks, keeping them moist and tender. Prepared in this simple fashion, the veal is terrific paired with an Oregon pinot. Have little toasts or bread on hand to accommodate those who want to scoop out the marrow.

Serves 4

4 (2-inch-thick) meaty cross-cut veal shanks (about 1 pound each)
2 large yellow onions (about 1 pound)
5 to 6 plum tomatoes (about 1 1/4 pounds)
Salt
Freshly ground black pepper

Place the rack in the middle of the oven, and preheat the oven to 300°F.

Slice the onions into 1/4-inch-thick rings. Quarter the tomatoes lengthwise. Tie each shank securely with kitchen string to keep the meat attached to bone. Season with salt and pepper. In a Dutch oven just wide enough to hold the shanks in one layer, toss together the onions and tomatoes and season with salt and pepper. Add the shanks and braise, covered, until they are very tender, about 2 1/2 to 3 hours.

The shanks may be made up to this point two days ahead and cooled, uncovered, before being chilled separately, covered. Reheat the shanks before proceeding.

Transfer the shanks, onions, and tomatoes to a platter with a slotted spoon and cover loosely to keep warm. Boil the braising liquid until it has reduced to about 1 cup, about 5 minutes. Season the jus to taste with salt and pepper.

Serve the shanks, onions, and tomatoes on top of mashed potatoes or creamy cheese grits, and perhaps a side of seared greens.

"Wine is the most healthful and most hygienic of beverages."

—LOUIS PASTEUR

WINE PAIRING
Willakenzie Estate
2004 Triple Black Slope
Pinot Noir

char grilled steak
with truffled potato salad

from Chef William King

Always start with a great steak! (Your favorite cut is a safe choice.) I prefer steaks on the bone like a cowboy rib-eye or, as in this recipe, a porterhouse T-bone. It's the potato salad that makes this meal extra special—creamy, rich, and gently perfumed with truffle oil. Potato salad is rarely considered elegant, but this one truly is.

Serves 4

For the steak:
2 (24- to 28-ounce) porterhouse steaks
4 tablespoons extra virgin olive oil
4 teaspoons Montreal seasoning

Coat the steaks with the oil and season well. Char over a hot fire, lower the temperature, and continue grilling to desired doneness. Allow them to rest for 2 to 3 minutes, then slice and serve with the potato salad, sprinkled with the chopped chives.

For the potato salad:
3 extra-large russet baking potatoes
3/4 cup mayonnaise
2 egg yolks
1 to 2 teaspoons truffle oil, depending on quality and flavor
1/4 teaspoon salt
1/4 teaspoon cracked black pepper
2 tablespoons chopped chives
1/4 cup julienne yellow onion
1/2 cup julienne celery

Peel and cut the potatoes into what the French refer to as buton cuts. These are rectangular blocks about 1 1/2 inches long by 1/2-inch square. (This step is optional, but it gives the salad a more elegant look.) Cook the potatoes in heavily salted, boiling water until just barely cooked. Be careful not to overcook. They should be just tender to the bite. Drain and rinse the potatoes in cold water.

Meanwhile, blend the mayonnaise, egg yolks, truffle oil, slant, pepper, and chives to form the dressing. Combine the potatoes, onion, and celery. Add the dressing, folding and blending well to coat. This salad is best when served not too cold. If you prepare it in advance, put it in the refrigerator, but allow it to warm up a bit at room temperature before serving.

swedish meatballs in dijon cream

from Scott Paul Wines

This recipe merges a traditional dish inspired by Scott Wright's Swedish heritage with a French-inspired mustard sauce. Serve over buttered noodles for an entrée or use as part of an hors d'oeuvre presentation.

Makes 60 small meatballs

Meatballs:
1 1/2 pound ground beef
1/2 pound ground pork (Ask your butcher to grind together the ground beef and ground pork.)
1 cup soft bread crumbs
1/2 cup half-and-half
4 tablespoons minced onion
1 teaspoon prepared mustard
1 tablespoon ketchup
1/2 teaspoon allspice
1/4 teaspoon cardamom
2 teaspoons salt
1/2 teaspoon freshly ground black pepper
2 tablespoons butter

Dijon cream sauce:
2 to 3 tablespoons diced shallots
3/4 cup dry white wine
3/4 cup reduced-sodium chicken stock
1/4 cup whipping cream
2 tablespoons Dijon mustard
1 tablespoon freshly chopped chives

To prepare the meatballs, soak the bread crumbs in the half-and-half. Add the onion, mustard, ketchup, allspice, cardamom, salt, and pepper and, using your hands, mix into the meat, until well incorporated.

Shape into small balls, not much bigger than 1 tablespoon each. Melt the butter in a skillet. In three batches, add the meatballs, turning occasionally, until they are brown on all sides, and just cooked through. Remove the meat balls from pan and place them on a paper towel-lined plate.

To prepare the sauce, add the shallots, wine, and stock to the same skillet used for the meatballs. Bring the liquid to a boil and reduce for 2 to 3 minutes. Add the cream, and allow to simmer and thicken. Stir in the mustard and chives.

Pass the Dijon cream in a gravy boat alongside the meatballs.

Chef's note: Any meatballs not being served right away can be frozen on a sheet pan, and then packed into a freezer bag. Thawed meatballs can be warmed in a skillet with butter or gravy.

roast prime rib of beef
with dijon mustard crust

from Erath Winery

This recipe is a bit unconventional, but the results are delicious. If you need an alternative prime rib and potatoes recipe, here it is. The dark fruit flavors and subtle hints of spice in Erath's Oregon Pinot Noir inspired long-time Erath employee Tim McGinnis to create these hearty dishes that utilize the wine.

Serves 4 to 6

1 (3 to 4-rib) roast
1/2 to 1 (8-ounce) jar Dijon mustard
1 cup kosher salt
1 to 1 1/2 cups Erath Oregon Pinot Noir, any vintage

Preheat the oven to 325°F.

Place the roast, fat-side-up, on a rack in a shallow roasting pan. Rub the outside of the entire roast with Dijon mustard, and press the kosher salt onto the roast. Pour the wine into the pan. Roast for 20 minutes per pound until desired doneness is reached. (140°F internal temperature for rare, 155°F internal temperature for medium-well.)

Erath Pinot Noir potatoes:
1 to 2 pounds small, whole red potatoes
2 cups Erath Oregon Pinot Noir
1 shallot, diced
2 cloves garlic, minced
1 teaspoon kosher salt
1/2 to 1 cube of butter

Parboil the potatoes until they are fork-tender. Dice the potatoes to 1 inch and reserve. Pour 2 cups of the wine into a large frying pan, and add the shallot and garlic. Reduce by half over medium heat. Season with the salt, and finish the sauce with 1/2 to 1 cube of butter. Add the potatoes and heat through. Serve with the prime rib roast.

oregon pinot noir camp

Each year a unique event occurs in Oregon. Very low key, some might say…secretly. It is the Oregon Pinot Noir Camp, a super-exclusive event held for the benefit of professionals in the wine and restaurant industry from around the world. This is serious stuff! The wine camp includes educational events, seminars, and tastings, with workshops that cover everything, from soil and agricultural practices to climate and its impact on that year's vintage, to insight into flavor profiles, pairings, and promotional opportunities. It is "Boot Camp" for the wine world, Oregon-style. To my knowledge, there is nothing quite like it anywhere in the world. (But of course, I could say that about Oregon in general and specifically about our wines!)

WINE PAIRING
Penner-Ash Wine Cellars
2006 Willamette Valley
Pinot Noir

braised short ribs of beef

from Penner-Ash Wine Cellars

The rich, almost Bourbon quality of a good stout beer enhances the savory elements of this slow-cook short-rib recipe from Gourmet Magazine (March 2005). A converted fan of braising meats, Ron Penner-Ash enjoys the easy pace of an early morning preparation, which allows him, as the cook, to engage with guests without frantic, last-minute issues. There's nothing sweeter than a perfectly seasoned short rib flaking off the bone with the light touch of your fork!

Serves 4 to 6

4 to 4 1/4 pound beef short ribs, cut into 4-inch pieces
1/4 cup packed dark brown sugar
1 tablespoon sweet paprika
1 tablespoon curry powder
2 teaspoons ground cumin
2 teaspoons freshly ground black pepper
2 teaspoons salt
1 teaspoon dry mustard
4 medium leeks (white and pale green parts only), chopped
3 tablespoons olive oil
4 medium carrots, chopped
3 stalks celery, chopped
2 Turkish bay leaves (or 1 California)
1/4 cup chopped garlic
1 3/4 cups beef broth
3 (12-ounce) bottles stout beer
2 (14-ounce) cans diced tomatoes

Place the oven rack in the lower third of the oven and preheat to 375°F.

Stir together the brown sugar, paprika, curry powder, cumin, pepper, salt, and mustard in a small bowl until combined.

Pat the ribs dry and arrange in one layer in a shallow baking pan or a shallow dish, then generously coat all sides of the ribs with the spice mixture. Marinate, uncovered and chilled, 1 hour.

Clean the leeks by rinsing in cold water.

Heat the oil in a pot over high heat until it is hot, but not smoking. Quickly brown the ribs on all 3 meaty sides without crowding, in batches if necessary, about 1 minute per side. Transfer the meat to a large plate, then add the leeks, carrots, celery, and bay leaves and cook over low heat, stirring occasionally, until the vegetables begin to soften, about 3 minutes. Add the garlic and continue to cook, stirring, for 1 minute.

Add the broth, beer, and tomatoes with their juice, then add the ribs with any juices and remaining spices accumulated on the plate. Bring the liquid to a boil, uncovered. Cover the pot and transfer to the oven, then braise until meat is very tender, about 3 hours.

pork & lamb

My favorite recipes reside in this section. I love pork and lamb in almost any form! These dishes will not disappoint. The rich, full flavors they create are the ideal matches for Oregon's fabulous repertoire of Pinot noirs.

garlic glazed pork chops
with marsala red wine reduction

from Chef William King

I don't know which I love more: grilled pork, roasted pork, cured pork, braised pork…you get the idea. For the grilled pork fans, this is a favorite recipe that builds flavor on the meat and then adds complementary flavors with the sauce, the foundation of which is a good Oregon Pinot noir. This recipe is one of my favorites to use for the fabulous thick pork chops I get from my friends at Carlton Pork Farms.

Serves 4

4 (14-ounce) center-cut rib pork chops
12 large cloves of garlic
1/2 cup extra virgin olive oil
1 tablespoon cracked black pepper
1 tablespoon Montreal seasoning
1 tablespoon freshly chopped rosemary
1/2 tablespoon freshly chopped thyme

1/2 bottle Oregon Pinot noir
1 medium yellow onion, diced
1 cup Marsala wine
1 cup rich chicken stock
1/2 cup rich beef stock
1/4 cup honey

Combine the garlic, olive oil, pepper, Montreal seasoning, rosemary and thyme. Purée to a rough, paste-like consistency. Place the chops in a large bowl, add the purée, and toss to coat thoroughly. Allow to rest for at least 3 to 4 hours, or overnight.

Place the pinot in a saucepan and reduce over medium heat by one-half. You will be left with about one cup of wine.

While the wine is reducing, brown the onions in another pan with a little oil, then reduce the heat and simmer to caramelize, about fifteen minutes. Add the reduced wine, Marsala, both stocks, and honey to the onions and simmer another twenty minutes or so to reduce by half. You will be left with about 2 to 2 1/2 cups of sauce. Strain and reserve.

Heat a grill or barbecue to very hot. Scrape most of the marinade off the pork chops, as it will burn if you do not. Don't worry, the flavor will remain. Grill the chops to a dark, charred color then reduce the heat or move them to a cooler part of the grill to finish. If you prefer, you can put them in a 350°F oven to finish for 10 minutes or so.

If you like to use a thermometer to judge doneness, cook the chops to 130°F internal temperature. Let them rest for 5 to 7 minutes before serving. They will be just about a perfect medium, 140°F internal.

While the chops are cooling, return the sauce to a medium heat and reduce further. The final consistency should be lightly thickened and syrupy. If you finish the chops in the oven, be sure to add any accumulated juices from the pan to the sauce.

Place one chop on each guest's plate and spoon a generous 3 to 4 tablespoons of the sauce over each. Serve with your favorite accompaniments. In the fall and winter, I like to serve them with a butternut squash gratin and fresh apple, celery-root slaw.

pork tenderloin
with strawberry rhubarb purée

from Bethel Heights Vineyard

The window is narrow, but in mid- to late-June both the world's best strawberries and rhubarb are available at the same time for a couple of weeks. It's the perfect time to prepare this delicious pork. The tart, piquant flavors of the sauce balance nicely with the rich, sweet flavor of the tenderloin.

Serves 4

3 pork tenderloins, approximately 1 pound each
1 1/2 pounds fresh rhubarb, cut in small chunks
1/4 cup honey (more to taste)
1/2 cup red wine
2 tablespoons Dijon-style mustard
1/4 cup rich chicken stock (or veal stock)
1 cup fresh ripe strawberries, stemmed, diced
2 tablespoons cold butter, cut in small pieces
2 tablespoons olive oil
Salt
Fresh ground black pepper

Preheat the oven to 350°F.

To prepare the strawberry-rhubarb purée, bring the diced rhubarb, honey, wine, mustard, and broth to a low boil and cook, uncovered, until the rhubarb falls apart and the sauce thickens slightly. Stir often. When the rhubarb is mostly cooked down, add the strawberries and continue to simmer until the berries are very soft. At this point, adjust for sweetness, adding 2 to 3 tablespoons of additional honey if the sauce is too tart. Season to taste with salt and pepper. Reserve. Add any juices from the roasted pork to the sauce, and reheat just before serving. If desired, swirl in some butter for added richness.

To prepare the pork tenderloins, grill or brown the meat on top of the stove over medium heat in olive oil. Season to taste with salt and pepper. Place the meat on a rack in a roasting pan, and cook for about 20 minutes, until an instant-read thermometer registers 165°F. The meat should be slightly pink in the center. Remove and let stand, loosely covered, for 15 minutes while reheating the sauce.

To serve, slice the meat and lay in overlapping pieces on a pool of sauce. Serve this dish with roasted asparagus or green beans and grilled polenta to take advantage of seasonal fruit and vegetable combinations.

Optional: If you like your sauce perfectly smooth, it can be puréed in a food processor before reheating.

WINE PAIRING
RoxyAnn Winery
Hillcrest Orchard
Pear Wine

medallions of pork

with caramelized pears and pear wine cream sauce

from RoxyAnn Winery

Pears are Oregon's signature tree fruit and a beautiful addition to this pork tenderloin dish from RoxyAnn Winery. This is a fairly rich entrée but very delicious and great for a fall evening.

Serves 4

1 (1 1/4-pound) pork tenderloin, trimmed, cut crosswise into 1-inch-thick slices
Salt
Freshly ground black pepper
4 tablespoons butter, divided
4 firm, but ripe Anjou or Bartlett pears, peeled, halved, cored, cut into 1/3-inch-thick wedges
1 teaspoon sugar
2 tablespoons cooking oil

Pear wine cream sauce:
1/2 cup chopped shallots
1 1/4 teaspoon dried thyme
1/4 cup Hillcrest Orchard pear wine (or pear brandy)
1 cup whipping cream
1/3 cup pear juice, such as Knudsen's® (or pear nectar)

Place the pork slices between plastic wrap. Using a meat mallet, pound the slices to 1/4-inch thickness. Season both sides with salt and pepper.

Melt 2 tablespoons of the butter in a large, non-stick skillet or sauté pan over high heat. Add the pears and the sugar. Sauté until the pears are tender and deep-golden, about 8 minutes.

Melt 1 tablespoon of butter along with the oil in another large, nonstick skillet or sauté pan over high heat. Working in batches, add pork to the skillet, and sauté just until cooked through, about 2 minutes. Transfer to a plate, and cover with foil to keep warm.

Reduce the heat in the pan to medium. Melt the additional 1 tablespoon of butter in the same skillet. Add the shallots and thyme, and sauté for 2 minutes. Add the pear wine, and boil until the mixture is reduced to a glaze, scraping up any browned bits, about 2 minutes. Add the cream and pear juice, and reduce until thickened to a sauce consistency, about 5 minutes. Season to taste with salt and pepper.

Reheat the pears if necessary. Place 2 to 3 medallions of pork on individual plates. Serve the pears alongside the pork. Pour the sauce over the pork, and serve.

WINE PAIRING
Cristom Vineyards
2005 Marjorie Vineyard
Pinot Noir

pomegranate and spiced braised pork

from Cristom Vineyards

Here's a very interesting braised pork recipe utilizing full flavors and lots of spice. The sauce produced from the braising liquid is a perfect foil to the rich meat of the pork shoulder. John D'Anna from Cristom adapted this recipe from an article by Lynne Char Bennett that appeared in the San Francisco Chronicle in 2004, and it has been a favorite at the winery ever since.

Serves 6

3 1/2 to 4 pounds bone-in pork shoulder roast
Kosher salt
Freshly ground pepper
4 teaspoons vegetable oil
1 large onion, chopped
5 large cloves garlic, peeled, smashed
6 slices fresh ginger, 1/8-inch thick, and about the size of a quarter
2 star anise

1 stick cinnamon, about 2 inches long
2 teaspoons whole black peppercorns
2 cups dry, fruity red wine
2 cups unsweetened pomegranate juice
1/2 cup soy sauce
2 teaspoons fish sauce
2 teaspoons hoisin sauce
2 tablespoons dark brown sugar, or more

Season all sides of the pork with salt and pepper. Heat 2 teaspoons of the oil in a skillet over medium-high heat. Add the meat, and sear until dark golden-brown, turning as necessary. Remove the meat from the skillet and set aside.

Heat the remaining 2 teaspoons of oil in a Dutch oven just large enough to hold the roast. Add the onion, and sauté until translucent, then add the garlic and cook until aromatic.

Add the ginger, star anise, cinnamon, and peppercorns. Place the pork in the Dutch oven and add the wine, pomegranate juice, soy sauce, fish sauce, and hoisin. The liquid should come at least halfway up on the roast. If not, add more wine and pomegranate juice (in equal amounts) or water.

Stir, cover, and bring to a simmer. Check the level of tartness after 30 minutes, then add brown sugar if needed to balance the acidity of the wine and tartness of the juice.

Continue cooking at a low simmer for another hour, then turn the roast and simmer for about 1 1/2 hours or more, or until the meat is fork-tender.

Remove the meat to a platter and keep warm. Bring the sauce to a boil and reduce by about 1/4 to 1/2. Strain and discard the solids. Remove the bone from the meat (it should easily release on its own), and cut the meat into serving portions. Return the meat to the sauce to rewarm, if needed, then serve, spooning the sauce over the meat.

Note: The roast can be made ahead and reheated. The flavors meld and the meat becomes more intensely flavored as it rests overnight in the sauce—especially if the meat is sliced or shredded first.

stuffed pork loin
with balsamic glaze and tempranillo reduction

from Abacela

Tempranillo, a rather distinguished gentleman of a wine, certainly deserves a recipe of equal stature that features classic Spanish cuisine paired with some New-World ingenuity like stuffed pork loin with balsamic glaze and Tempranillo reduction.

Serves 4 to 6

1 medium-sized (3 to 3 1/2 pound) pork loin, butterflied about 1-inch thick (Get the big loin, not the smaller tenderloin.)
1 1/2 cups cantimpalo (a coarsely ground chorizo-style sausage), diced into small pieces (or linguica)
1 large shallot, minced
3 cloves garlic, minced
1 tablespoon sweet paprika
Salt
Cracked black pepper

2 tablespoons extra virgin olive oil
3 tablespoons coarsely chopped fresh sage
3 tablespoons coarsely chopped fresh thyme
3 tablespoons coarsely chopped fresh parsley
1/2 cup balsamic vinegar
1 cup Abacela's 2002 Estate Tempranillo
1/2 stick butter, cut into pats
At least 1 wine glass
Wooden toothpicks

Submerge the toothpicks in a bowl of water for at least 10 minutes prior to using.

Lay the pork loin out on a flat surface.

Preheat the grill.

In a medium saucepan over medium heat, render the cantimpalo, then use a slotted spoon to remove it to drain, leaving the fat in the pan. Add the shallot, garlic, paprika, salt, cracked black pepper, and 1 tablespoon of the olive oil. Cook until just barely translucent.

Combine the sage, thyme, and parsley in a small bowl. Return the cantimpalo to the saucepan and add 3/4 of the fresh herb mixture. When the herbs have just wilted, take the stuffing off the heat. When cool, spread the stuffing evenly on the pork loin and roll it up. Pin it closed with the presoaked toothpicks.

Place the stuffed loin back in the pan on high heat and sear the outside in 2 tablespoons of balsamic vinegar. When the loin has browned on all sides, place it on the hot grill and glaze regularly with the remaining balsamic vinegar.

Taste the wine. Retaste the wine. Retaste the wine again if necessary. Deglaze the pan with the wine. When the wine has reduced by half, remove the pan from the heat, and let it cool until just warm enough to melt the butter. Add the butter and when melted, pour over the finished loin. Garnish with the remainder of the fresh herbs.

WINE PAIRING
RoxyAnn Winery
2005 Syrah

porchetta style roast pork loin
with winter fruits and vegetables

from Chef William King

This is a very impressive roast that will serve a large group. It also works well as a component for a winter holiday buffet. This is a spin-off of the Italian roasted suckling pig with sausage stuffing that is one of the country's most festive preparations. This meal can certainly be served in warmer months as well, with seasonal vegetable accompaniments.

Serves 12 or more

1/2 boneless pork loin, about 12 to 14 inches long
1 (12-ounce) package pitted prunes
1 1/2 cups port
1 1/2 cups Pinot noir
1/2 pound bulk sausage, sweet or hot Italian
1 to 2 tablespoons Montreal seasoning
6 tart apples, quartered
16 cups large diced root vegetables (potatoes, carrots, onions, etc.)
2 cups chicken stock
8 cloves garlic, peeled, roasted, puréed
Salt
Freshly ground black pepper

Soak the prunes in the port and pinot overnight.

Preheat the oven to 400°F.

Split or "butterfly" the pork loin by splitting it lengthwise. You can open it even further with additional lengthwise cuts until it is opened flat, like a jelly-roll cube. Spread the sausage over the cut surfaces and fold or roll the pork over the stuffing until it returns to its original shape. Tie the roast at 3 to 4-inch intervals with kitchen twine to hold it together. Tie it tightly so that the roast holds its shape and the sausage stays wrapped inside.

Season with Montreal seasoning and roast for 30 minutes. Reduce the heat to 325°F and continue roasting for about one hour, or until the internal temperature reaches 140°F. Allow the roast to rest 20 minutes before carving.

While the pork is roasting, roast the apples and vegetables either separately or in the same pan with the pork for the last 45 minutes. My favorite technique is to sear the vegetables in butter and/or oil over very high heat in a sauté pan to get a nice dark caramelized exterior on them. I finish them with the roast for about the last 20 minutes.

To make the sauce, drain the port and pinot off the prunes, resealing them until service. Place the wine, chicken stock, and the roasted garlic in a sauce pan and bring to a boil. Lower the heat to simmer and reduce the mixture to two cups. Add the pan juices to the wines while they are reducing. Season to taste with salt and pepper.

Carve the pork roast, exposing the attractive sausage stuffing, and surround it with the reserved prunes, apples, and roasted vegetables. Serve the sauce separately.

blue corn tamales
with serrano ham and goat cheese

from Abacela

This tamale recipe is not traditional but wow, what flavors! As winemaker Kiley Evans, who provided this recipe, said, "Place the tamales on a serving platter, drizzle with the sauce and get out of the way!"

Makes 12 to 15 tamales

Filling:
1 (1-pound) whole serrano ham (dry-cured Spanish ham), not sliced (or proscuitto)
1 (8-ounce) package dried corn husks
2 teaspoons thyme
2 teaspoons tarragon
2 teaspoons oregano
2 tablespoons extra virgin olive oil
1/2 large white onion, thinly sliced
2 cups veal stock (or beef stock)
4 cloves garlic

Sauce:
2 whole serrano chilis, about 3-inches long, destemmed
1 teaspoon ground cumin
8 ounces goat cheese
1/4 cup crème fraîche (or sour cream)

Dough:
2/3 cup lard
1/4 teaspoon chipotle powder or chili powder
1/2 teaspoon salt (This may not be needed if substituting prosciutto or other ham.)
1 teaspoon baking soda
2 cups blue-corn harinilla *(see page 183)*
1 cup veal stock (or beef stock)

Place the corn husks in a large bowl and cover with water until soft, at least 3 to 4 hours, turning occasionally. Another heavy bowl may have to be placed on top of the husks to keep them submerged.

To prepare the filling, combine the thyme, tarragon, and oregano in a small bowl. Heat the oil over medium-high heat in a medium-sized boiling pot. When hot, add in the onion, and cook until translucent. Add the ham, stock, half of the herb mixture, and the garlic. Bring to a boil and simmer for 30 to 40 minutes until the ham is falling apart. After simmering, remove the onion, garlic, and liquid to a blender. Shred the ham using two forks. Set the ham aside.

To prepare the sauce, preheat the broiler. Place the chilies on a foil-lined baking sheet and cook until the skin blackens in spots, turning once. Remove the chilies and any juices to the blender with the simmering liquid. Add the cumin and blend until smooth. Add the goat cheese and crème fraîche, and stir until melted in and smooth.

To prepare the dough, using an electric mixer, beat the lard, chipotle powder, salt, and baking soda until fluffy.   Add the harinilla flour in 1/2-cup batches. Once incorporated, reduce the speed to low, and slowly add in the stock until a soft, tender dough is formed. If the dough is too firm, add more stock in small increments (2 tablespoons at a time) until the dough is soft.

To assemble: Cut two (or more, if needed) husks into thin strips and tie one end of each remaining husk closed with a strip.

Lay the husks out, spread the dough on the husks to about 1/4 to 1/2-inch-thick, and then add a tablespoon of the ham in the center. Sprinkle with the remaining herb mixture, and fold the husk closed. Tie up the open end of the husk with another strip and set aside into a rice steamer or equivalent. Steam for 1 hour.

Remove from the steamer and untie one end of the husk, and drizzle with the sauce.

braised lamb shanks

from The Eyrie Vineyards

This is an adaptation from cookbook author, Tom Valenti. Jason Lett adds the cherries, braising them in the cooking juices, which adds a bit of sweetness to the savor and link the wine and the lamb together perfectly.

Serves 4 to 6

4 to 6 lamb shanks
Coarsely ground salt
Freshly ground black pepper
1/2 cup olive oil
3 cups mixed: chopped celery, carrot, and onion
1/2 cup tomato paste
5 sprigs thyme
1 bay leaf
1 tablespoon black peppercorns
1 whole head garlic, halved
4 cups red wine (See chef's note.)
1 cup dry white wine (See chef's note.)
1/3 cup white vinegar
1 teaspoon sugar
2 cups veal stock or 1 cup demi-glace
2 cups chicken stock
3 cups dried black cherries

Preheat the oven to 325°F.

Season the lamb shanks liberally with salt and pepper. With a sharp knife, cut about 1 inch from the bottom (narrow end) of the shank bones down to the bone and all the way around; this will help expose the bone while cooking. Reserve.

Heat 3 tablespoons of oil in a pot over medium-high heat. Add the celery, carrot, onion mix to the pot, and cook until very soft, about 8 to 10 minutes. Add the tomato paste, and cook for 1 to

2 minutes. Add the thyme, bay leaf, peppercorns, anchovies, and garlic, and cook for another 2 to 3 minutes. Add both the red and white wines, reserving 1 cup of the red for later. Add the vinegar, and sugar, raise the heat to high, and bring to a boil.

Lower the heat to medium and add the veal and chicken stock. Leave over medium heat while you brown the shanks.

In a sauté pan over high heat, brown the shanks well in the remaining 1/2 cup oil on all sides, until they are well browned.

Transfer the shanks to a roasting pan and pour the stock mixture on top. Cover with aluminum foil and cook in the preheated oven for 1 hour. Remove the foil and cook for another 3 hours, turning the shanks over every half hour until the meat is very soft. One hour before the shank is done, add the dried cherries and the reserved wine. Remove the shanks from the braising liquid and strain the liquid. Skim any fat that rises to the surface and use the liquid as a sauce.

Serve the shanks over rice, soft polenta or mashed potatoes, and liberally pour the strained, skinned stock over the top.

Chef's note: Use any good red or white wine that isn't Eyrie for preparing the dish. Save the Eyrie to drink with the lamb. You will have worked hard for it.

sineann grilled lamb
with smashed potatoes

from Sineann

Just a few ingredients, but all of wonderful freshness and quality. Plenty of garlic, rosemary, and great red wine are all you need when the lamb is Oregon lamb!

Serves 6 to 8

1 (5-pound) boneless leg of lamb, butterflied
6 cloves garlic
1 (20-leaf sprig) fresh rosemary
1/4 cup of tamari or soy sauce
4 tablespoons olive oil
2 cups red wine
Salt
Freshly ground black pepper

Peel and chop the garlic. Place in a bowl large enough to hold the leg of lamb. Pull the leaves off of the rosemary sprig, and place them in the bowl. Add the tamari, olive oil, and wine. Place the leg of lamb in the bowl, turning to coat it fully. (You can leave this marinating for any number of hours—from a few to overnight—covered, in the refrigerator.) Submerge or turn occasionally for uniform distribution of the marinade.

Start a good-sized bed of coals in a barbeque that can cook enclosed. When the coals are hot, distribute them around the perimeter of the grill's bowl, leaving a small, dinner-plate-sized opening in the middle. Place a pan or some folded-up aluminum foil in a crude, bowl-shape in the opening. (The idea is to create a place for the fat to drip off the lamb without falling on the coals, which causes flare ups.)

Place the grill back in place, and lay the leg of lamb over this area. Salt and pepper the lamb, and put the cover back onto the grill.

Grill until a meat thermometer registers about 135°F in the thickest part of the meat. This will give you some pink meat. You can adjust the doneness according to your preference by removing the meat when the thermometer registers at a higher or lower temperature. There will be a mixture of well-done and medium-rare by removing the meat when it reaches about 135°F.

Smashed Potatoes:
Any number of small, tasty potatoes (The Rosback family prefers Yukon Golds or Yellow Finns.)
Olive oil
Salt
Freshly ground black pepper

Preheat the oven to 375°F.

Clean the potatoes thoroughly. Place them in a pot big enough to cover the potatoes with water. Bring to a boil, and simmer for about 20 minutes until fork-tender. Drain.

Place individual potatoes between sheets of waxed paper and flatten to about a half an inch thick. Place on a cookie sheet, or similar cooking tray, placing several drops of olive oil under each smashed potato. Drizzle the tops with a bit more olive oil. Season to taste with salt and pepper. Place in the oven for 20 minutes. Remove the pan from the oven and turn the potatoes. Bake for another 20 minutes. Serve immediately.

This dish goes well with lamb, and just about anything else off the grill!

pork sausage sandwich
with fresh mozzarella, roasted tomatoes and red onion-pine nut relish

from Chef William King

Like almost everything, this sandwich is only as good as the ingredients you use. A great mild or spicy Italian sausage, a classic rustic crusty roll, and high-quality mozzarella make all the difference. This is a hearty sandwich just perfect for big appetites!

Serves 4

4 Fresh Italian sausages, hot or mild
4 Roma tomatoes
1/4 cup toasted pine nuts
1/4 cup minced red onion
2 tablespoons minced sun-dried tomatoes
2 tablespoons freshly chopped basil
2 tablespoons extra virgin olive oil
2 tablespoons tomato sauce, homemade or your favorite store-bought
Pinch salt
Freshly ground black pepper
4 sandwich rolls, about 6-inches long
Extra virgin olive oil, to brush the bread
12 slices fresh mozzarella cheese
6 tablespoons mayonnaise, preferably homemade

Preheat the oven to 350°F.

Slice each tomato lengthwise into 3 to 4 slices, depending on how big they are, you want to end up with 1/2-inch-thick slices. Place them on a foil-lined baking sheet, and roast them in the oven for about 1 to 1 1/2 hours. They should be browned and reduced, but not dried out. Cool completely.

Combine the pine nuts, red onion, sun-dried tomatoes, basil, olive oil, tomato sauce, salt, and pepper, and blend well to form the red onion-pine nut relish. Reserve.

Cook the sausage in the manner you prefer: roast, pan-fry, grill, or boil. Place the mozzarella slices on the sausages, and allow the cheese to melt slightly in the oven or under the broiler. Split and brush the rolls with olive oil. Toast them in a pan, under the broiler, or on the grill.

To assemble: spread the rolls with the mayonnaise. Place the sausage and tomato slices in the rolls, and top with the red onion-pine nut relish. Serve with chips, fries, or a nice potato or pasta salad.

poultry & game

From versatile chicken, to richly flavored duck, to the wonderful, but underutilized and underappreciated bison or buffalo, we offer recipes that suit a variety of occasions. This is a very interesting group of dishes to pair wines with, as anything from rosé to Pinot noir can be matched with some of these preparations. Experiment and enjoy!

braised chicken
with peppers and ham

from Elk Cove Vineyards

This is a delicious example of traditional chicken and peppers that comes together easily in a baking dish and finishes nicely with rich, salty ham. Accompany it with saffron or herb-baked rice.

Serves 4 to 6

2 large free-range chickens, cut into serving pieces (Save the neck and back for future use.)
2 free-range chicken breasts, halved
Coarsely ground sea salt
Freshly ground black pepper
1 tablespoon olive oil
1 cup finely chopped shallots
4 cloves garlic, finely chopped
1 (25-ounce) can whole tomatoes
1 cup Oregon white wine, preferably pinot gris
2 cups low-sodium chicken broth (or homemade chicken broth)
3 sprigs thyme
2 sprigs marjoram
1/4 cup Spanish or country ham, diced to 1/4-inch

Preheat the oven to 375°F.

Season the chicken generously with the salt and pepper. Heat the olive oil over medium-high heat in a large Dutch oven, and braise the chicken pieces until they are well browned.

Place the chicken in a large baking dish or ovenproof pot. Pour off all of the oil except for 1 tablespoon. Add the shallots, and sauté for 5 minutes. Add the garlic, and sauté for 1 more minute. Add the tomatoes and wine and boil rapidly for 1 minute to vaporize the alcohol. Pour over the chicken. Add the chicken broth and herb sprigs to the chicken and cover with a lid or tin foil. Place in the oven, and roast for 30 minutes.

Remove the breasts, and roast the remaining pieces for an additional 30 minutes. Remove the chicken pieces to a large serving platter and keep warm. Pour the liquid from the baking dish into a stove-top-safe pot, and boil rapidly, reducing the liquid to 1 1/2 to 2 cups.

While the chicken is baking, prepare the pepper mixture.

Pepper mixture:
1 tablespoon olive oil
1 large red bell pepper, chopped
1 large yellow bell pepper, chopped
2 poblano peppers, chopped
4 cloves garlic, finely chopped
1 teaspoon mild paprika
1/4 cup freshly chopped Italian parsley
2 tablespoons freshly chopped marjoram

Heat the olive oil over medium-high heat in a large frying pan. Sauté the peppers in olive oil for 5 minutes, or until lightly colored. Add the garlic and paprika, and cook for 1 minute. Set aside.

Just before serving, add the pepper mixture to the liquid and heat through. Add the parsley and marjoram. Pour the liquid over the chicken, and sprinkle with the ham cubes.

pinot braised chicken
in the style of coq au vin

from Chef William King

Coq au Vin is one of the greatest dishes of French cuisine. This Pacific Northwest version is equally wonderful, taking full advantage of local products, with Pinot noir as the star of the show

Serves 4

2 large (4 to 5-pound) roasting chickens, cut into quarters or eights
1 tablespoon salt
1 tablespoon cracked black pepper
1/2 cup vegetable oil
1 bottle Pinot noir
1/2 pound thick-sliced bacon, cut into 1-inch pieces
1/2 pound button mushrooms, quartered
1/2 pound pearl onions, fresh, peeled, blanched (or frozen)
3 cups demi glace
2 tablespoons butter

Season the chicken pieces with salt and pepper. Brown them in the oil over medium heat in a large sauté pan. Meanwhile, reduce the wine by half in a separate sauce pan. When the chicken is well browned on all sides, transfer the chicken pieces to a large Dutch oven or deep roasting pan in a single layer.

Return the sauté pan to the heat and cook the bacon until browned, but not crisp. Remove the bacon from the pan and reserve. Keep the bacon fat in the pan and sauté the mushrooms and onions in the bacon fat.

Combine the reduced wine with the demi glace and pour over the chicken to cover. The chicken may be cooked, covered, on top of the stove over low heat, or in a 325°F oven. After about 20 to 30 minutes, when the chicken is just barely done, add the bacon, mushrooms and onions, and continue cooking for an additional 10 to 15 minutes.

Remove the chicken pieces to a serving platter, swirl the butter into the sauce, and pour it over the chicken. Serve with your favorite accompaniment. I love this with soft polenta, but you can also serve this with rice, risotto, or egg noodles.

chicken breasts
with parmesan-herbed bread crumbs

from Stoller Vineyards

This recipe is extremely versatile! It can be prepared with almost any chicken, fish, or even pork tenderloin, using whole-wheat bread crumbs, crushed crackers, or panko bread crumbs. Use your creativity, and substitute whatever herbs are fresh and in season. This dish pairs nicely with a wide variety of wines, depending on the type of meat and herbs used.

Serves 4

4 skinless, boneless chicken breasts, halved
1 clove garlic, peeled
1/4 cup Herbs de Provence
1/2 cup whole-wheat bread crumbs
1/4 cup grated Parmesan cheese
2 tablespoons olive oil
1/4 teaspoon kosher salt
Freshly ground black pepper
4 teaspoons Dijon mustard
Cooking spray

Preheat the oven to 400°F.

Lightly coat a baking dish with cooking spray. Mince the garlic in a small food processor, then add the Herbs de Provence, and pulse until combined, about 15 seconds. Add the bread crumbs, Parmesan, olive oil, salt, and a few grinds of black pepper. Pulse until well combined.

Arrange the chicken in the baking dish. Spread each chicken breast with a teaspoon of Dijon mustard, and pat the crumb mixture on top. Bake until cooked through, about 25 minutes.

quick facts

Oregon is the third largest wine-producing state in the country behind California and Washington. With over 14,000 acres planted as vineyards, more than 300 wineries, producing over 1.6 million cases annually, Oregon's wine industry generates over $1.5 billion in annual sales! From very small operations that produce fewer than 200 cases a year, to the "Big Hitters," whose output exceeds 100,000 cases annually, Oregon's world-class Pinot noirs lead the way, with Pinot gris coming in second. Other varietals are now contributing to tremendous growth throughout the seven growing regions as well.

duck with edenvale syrah

from EdenVale Winery

If you want to follow the instructions for boning a duck, I applaud you. If not, legs and boned breasts can be purchased separately at specialty meat markets. Or, you can ask a butcher to bone the duck for you. However you end up with the finished pieces, they will go beautifully with this sauce from EdenVale. It requires several hours of reduction in stages, but is well worth the effort.

Serves 4 to 8

2 whole ducks, thawed in the refrigerator (Discard the liver, or reserve for another use. Reserve the neck, heart and gizzard to be roasted with the bones.)
1 head garlic, split (Reserve and finely chop some of the cloves for the finished sauce.)
2 cups chicken stock
2 large yellow onions, peeled, coarsely chopped
2 large carrots, scraped, coarsely chopped
4 large ribs of celery, leaves minimized, coarsely chopped
2 bay leaves
1 bottle of EdenVale Syrah, divided
1 tablespoon coarsely ground fennel seeds
1 teaspoon freshly minced parsley
1 teaspoon freshly minced thyme
1 tablespoon kosher salt
1 tablespoon coarsely ground black peppercorns

To bone the duck:
Remove the breasts by following along either side of the breast bone with your sharpest knife, staying as close to the wishbone as possible. Continue to slice down along the ribs until the breast is freed from the carcass. Repeat on the other side, and trim the excess skin from around the breast leaving 1/4-inch of the skin surrounding the meat.

Flip the duck over and remove the legs, first popping the hip ball out of its socket, then freeing the leg from the body with your knife. Place the breasts and legs in the refrigerator.

Continued on the next page...

duck with edenvale syrah *continued...*

Syrah reduction, part I:
Preheat the oven to 400°F.

Roast the carcass bones and the garlic head in a 2-inch deep roasting pan until it is toffee brown. Pour off the excess fat and de-glaze the pan with chicken stock, scraping the brown reduction from the bottom of the roasting pan.

Place the bones, the deglazing liquid, and all the bits scraped from the roasting pan, along with the vegetables and bay leaves in a stockpot, barely cover with water and simmer for 4 to 6 hours. Strain the stock and refrigerate overnight.

To prepare the legs:
Preheat the oven to 400°F.

Remove the solidified fat from the stock. Reserve cold.

Place the stock in a saucepan and simmer, skimming until reduced by half.

While the stock is reducing, roast the duck legs, skin-side-up, in the oven for about 45 minutes, or until crisp. Add the stock and 1/2 bottle of the Syrah to the roasting pan, so it comes 3/4 of the way up the duck legs, but does not cover them. Continue to roast/braise the legs until fork-tender, about another hour. Remove the legs and hold warm.

Syrah reduction, part II:
Return the braising liquid to a saucepan, add the remaining 1/2 bottle of Syrah and the remaining herbs, salt, pepper, and the reserved chopped garlic, and reduce the liquid to a thickened, syrupy consistency.

To prepare the breasts:
While the legs rest and the sauce reduces, prepare the breasts. Heat 1 to 2 tablespoons of the reserved duck fat in a hot sauté pan. Place the breasts, skin-side-down, in the pan to brown the skin.

Drain off most of the fat, turn the breasts over, add the legs and any juices that have collected from them to the pan, and continue to cook over low heat for 3 to 4 minutes. The breasts are done when medium to medium-rare.

Serve the duck with your favorite accompaniments. (I like roasted potatoes and seasonal vegetables.) Strain the Syrah reduction over the plated duck.

"EdenVale Syrah is a wine produced in the Rogue Valley of southern Oregon, with grapes sourced from multiple vineyards across this diverse and developing wine growing area. The complex and multifaceted varietal character of the Syrah grape is exemplified by blending wines from vineyards in different microclimates."

—PATRICK FALLON, EdenVale Winery winemaker

grilled molasses-marinated quail
with frisée and tapenade

from Archery Summit

There is plenty of flavor in this recipe from Chef Eric Mazko. Semi-boneless quail are not easy to find in retail markets. In the restaurant world, we have a great source for this product—Nicky USA. Even if you use another type of poultry, this is a tasty, interesting recipe and could be a dinner or an elegant lunch.

Serves 6

6 semi-boneless quails
1 tablespoon olive oil, plus extra as needed
2 tablespoons light molasses
1 teaspoon freshly chopped garlic
2 teaspoons freshly chopped thyme
1 ounce Archery Summit Arcus Pinot Noir
Salt
Freshly ground black pepper
2 bundles frisée, green parts removed
1 tablespoon red wine ver-jus

Tapenade:
1/2 cup pitted niçoise olives
1 anchovy fillet, rinsed
1 teaspoon capers
1 tablespoon basil, sliced chiffonade
1 clove garlic
Olive oil

Combine the olive oil, molasses, garlic, thyme, wine, and quails in a small bowl. Toss to coat. Cover, and refrigerate for at least 8 hours, preferably overnight.

For the tapenade, combine the olives, anchovies, capers, basil, and garlic in a food processor. Add the olive oil in a steady stream while processing until the mixture becomes a coarse paste. Stop if the oil seems to "break" or fail to emulsify. This tapenade can also sit overnight.

Prepare the grill to high heat. Remove the quails from the marinade and pat dry with paper towels. Season each with salt and pepper, then grill each quail, turning only once. Remove the quails from the heat, but keep warm while resting.

Toss the frisée with half of the tapenade and red wine ver-jus. Add salt and pepper to taste. To plate, place greens in the center and top with quail. Garnish with additional tapenade.

enchiladas suiza

from Ponzi Vineyards

This recipe comes from Nancy Ponzi's extensive study of Mexican cooking. As both a student in Mexico City and a teacher here in Portland, Nancy has been inspired by the true nature of this wonderful cuisine and offers these enchiladas, which blend Mexican and European influences.

Serves 4 to 6

2 cups coarsely chopped, cooked chicken
1 medium onion, chopped
2 tablespoons vegetable oil
1 clove garlic, finely chopped
1 cup tomato purée with chopped tomato
2 or more mild green chilies, chopped
Salt
Freshly ground black pepper
3 cups sweet cream (or half-and-half)
6 chicken bouillon cubes
12 corn tortillas
Vegetable oil, for frying
1/2 pound coarsely grated Cotija or Monterey Jack cheese

For optional garnish:
Additional warm tortillas
Sliced avocado
Hard-cooked eggs
Radishes cut into flowers
Assorted salsas (Too many hot chilies can destroy the delicacy of this dish and the wine.)

Preheat the oven to 350°F.

Arrange an assembly line for cooking, dipping, filling and baking. Keep everything in sequence and the result is delicious, aromatic, and fun.

Sauté the onion in vegetable oil. When the onion is soft, add the garlic and cook for a bit longer, being careful not to burn the garlic. Add the chicken, tomato purée, green chilies, salt, and pepper. Adjust the seasonings to taste (may need more chili) and reserve.

For the sauce, heat the cream in a flat-bottomed sauté pan, but don't allow it to boil. Add the bouillon cubes, and stir until dissolved. Keep the sauce warm.

Cook the tortillas one by one, either by frying them in 1 inch of vegetable oil, or heating them lightly over the flame, turning with tongs just when they color and soften. As you heat them, dip each tortilla in the hot cream, place on a plate, and spoon a generous amount of filling down the center of the tortilla.

Roll the filled tortilla and place, seam-side-down, in a flat-bottomed baking dish. When the tortillas are rolled, cover with the remaining cream sauce, and top with the cheese. Bake for 30 minutes.

Chef's note: In Mexican cooking, the use of cream is associated with a dairy country; thus Suiza, which means Switzerland.

WINE PAIRING

Bethel Heights Vineyard
2006 Pinot Noir
Eola-Amity Hills Cuvée

roasted quail
with wine sauce and beet garnish

from Bethel Heights Vineyard

Quail benefit by air-drying overnight in the refrigerator. This ensures a nice dry bird that will brown well. Rinse the quail, pat them dry, place in a dish large enough to hold them, and refrigerate uncovered. I recommend buying semi-boned quail, as they are much easier to eat.

Serves 4 as a first course

4 semi-boneless quail
4 medium red beets, short stem and tail intact
1/2 cup freshly squeezed orange juice
8 tablespoons butter
4 shallots, minced
2 cups veal or chicken stock
1 cup red wine
1 cup seasonal berries, such as raspberries or blackberries (or frozen raspberries, thawed)
3 tablespoons olive oil
Salt
Freshly ground black pepper

Preheat the oven to 400°F.

To prepare the beet garnish, wash, but do not peel or cut the ends off of the beets. Pat dry and place in an 8 by 8-inch glass baking dish. Add the orange juice and 2 tablespoons of the butter. Cover tightly with foil and roast for 40 minutes, or until the beets pierce easily with a knife but are still firm. Let the beets cool in the juices. When they are slightly warm, remove the skins and place back in the beet liquid until ready to use. This may be done a day ahead and refrigerated, covered. When ready to serve, return to room temperature, remove from juices, and slice them evenly.

To prepare the wine sauce, combine the minced shallots with the stock and wine. Cook over medium-high heat until the liquid is reduced by half. Add the berries and reduce again. You should have 1 cup of liquid when the reductions are complete. Remove the sauce from the heat and strain, if necessary, to remove any seeds or skins from the berries. Cover, and reserve until ready to serve, then reheat briefly. Cut 4 tablespoons of the cold butter into small chunks and swirl into the re-heated sauce.

Brown the prepared quail evenly on both sides in olive oil and 2 tablespoons butter. This will take about 6 minutes. Season with salt and pepper, and place on a baking pan. Cut each bird in half lengthwise for best presentation. Reserve until you are ready to finish. To finish, roast, uncovered (400°F) for an additional 6 to 8 minutes, depending on the size of the birds. The meat juices should run clear when pricked with a fork.

To serve, fan two halves out on each plate, and drizzle sauce over each half. Garnish with beet slices.

cornish hen diavolo

from Chef William King

WINE PAIRING
Zerba Cellars
2003 Walla Walla Valley
Syrah

Mild and surprisingly flavorful, Cornish game hens make a great meal. They are miniature in size, so plan on serving one bird per person. This recipe produces a full-flavored, spicy, and crispy crust on the birds that is ideally created by either grilling or broiling. I recommend that you accompany the hens with soft polenta, a nice risotto, or, as shown here, piles of fresh, hot homemade french fries. Whatever else you choose, pick a full-bodied red wine that will stand up to the assertive, spicy flavors of the hen.

Serves 4

4 Cornish hens

For the marinade:
1 cup canola, soy, or vegetable oil
1 cup extra virgin olive oil
2 tablespoons Dijon mustard
1/4 cup Tabasco® Pepper Sauce
1 tablespoon crushed red chili flakes
2 tablespoons balsamic vinegar
2 tablespoons honey

Thaw and rinse the hens, removing the giblets for another use. Dry the hens well, then split down the back, remove the backbones, and flatten. Combine all the ingredients for the marinade and blend well. Marinate the hens for 3 to 4 hours or overnight.

For the rub:
2 tablespoons dried or fresh thyme
2 tablespoons dried or fresh oregano
1 tablespoon crushed red chili flakes
1 tablespoon Cajun spice
1 teaspoon Montreal seasoning

Combine the rub ingredients and blend well.

To assemble:
Heat the barbecue or grill with a hot fire. Or, optionally, preheat the broiler to 375°F in the oven.

Wipe the excess marinade off of the hens. Sprinkle them liberally with the rub mixture. Char the birds on both sides. The skin should be a nice dark brown. Finish the hens in the oven or, off the hot fire of the grill to a medium heat to cook through. Serve with your choice of accompaniment and be prepared to lick your fingers

terroir

Terroir is a very hip "buzz" word these days. A French word, literally translating to mean earth or dirt, terroir means much more than that in defining the sedimentary environment in which agricultural products grow. It is more about the characteristics that the environment imparts on those products. (The French terroir is the foundation of great wine making.) Currently in the United States, terroir is most often used in relationship to regional and/or local fruits and vegetables, in support of an overall culinary philosophy that supports the use of indigenous foods by markets and restaurants. In this context, it is Oregon's wine country—its terroir—and the relationship between the vineyards and garden crops, the winemakers and chefs that is fundamental to the region's commitment to blending, bonding, and celebrating all that we have been blessed with, and to making the most out of it.

Oregon's finest wine grapes are grown within a few miles of our most bountiful agricultural areas. In fact, they are all part of the same very rich and generous terroir that makes the state's bounty so unique and abundant. For chefs and vintners alike, this is a dream world in which to live and play.

fig-cured smoked duck breast

on baby spinach topped with duck skin cracklings,
rogue creamery blue cheese, and toasted oregon hazelnuts

from Trium

This is a rich and satisfying dish and a perfect complement to the Trium Growers' Cuvée with its layers of flavors and complexity. It showcases the best of Southern Oregon from the vineyard, creamery, and farm. The dressing is best if prepared a day ahead to allow the flavors to meld.

Serves 6

Cured and smoked duck:
6 duck breasts
3 cups fig juice
1/2 teaspoon freshly grated nutmeg
1 tablespoon salt
1/2 teaspoon freshly ground black pepper

Remove the skins from the duck breast. Place the skin flat on a waxed paper covered tray and freeze.

Mix the fig juice, nutmeg, salt, and pepper in a non-reactive pan. Place the duck breasts in single layer in the pan, making sure that they are completely submerged. Cover, and refrigerate at least overnight, preferably longer.

Prepare a very "soft" fire on the grill for slow smoking. Remove the breasts from the marinade. Smoke over hickory coals for 2 to 3 hours, until they are medium-rare. Baste occasionally with the marinade. Don't overcook the meat, it should be moist. Thinly slice the duck, and set aside. Refrigerate if not using immediately.

Caramelized shallot balsamic dressing:
3 shallots, peeled, diced
1 cup olive oil, plus 1 to 2 tablespoons
1/4 cup good-quality balsamic vinegar
1 teaspoon Dijon mustard
1 teaspoon Worcestershire sauce
6 ounces Rogue Creamery Blue cheese, crumbled
1 cup toasted and chopped Oregon hazelnuts

Caramelize the shallots in 1 to 2 tablespoons of the olive oil over medium-high heat. Cool and set aside.

Mix the olive oil, vinegar, mustard, and the Worcestershire. Season with salt and pepper. Add the shallots.

To assemble:
3 bunches baby spinach, cleaned
6 frozen duck skins
Salt
Freshly ground black pepper

Clean the baby spinach and set aside.

Remove the frozen duck skins from the freezer and immediately slice them into 1/4-inch- wide strips, the length of the skin. Render them in a heavy skillet until they are very crisp. Drain well. Season with salt and pepper and set aside.

Toss the baby spinach with vinaigrette and divide onto 6 plates. Top the spinach with slices of duck breast, crumbled blue cheese, toasted hazelnuts, and duck-skin cracklings.

Chef's note: Duck skins are much easier to cut while frozen. Separate, and cook slowly to avoid splatters. Save the rendered duck fat to use for other tasty frying.

WINE PAIRING
Ponzi Vineyards
2004 Pinot Gris

grilled chicken
with roasted vegetable "carpaccio"

from Chef William King

This dish is as much about presentation value as it is about flavor. The vegetables, carefully arranged in a colorful concentric pattern, produce a dramatic background to the flavorful, marinated chicken. I like this for a buffet, or as a grand mid-course in a lavish Italian meal. It is best prepared at the height of summer vegetable season.

Serves 4

For the chicken:
8 pieces whole, cut-up chicken (or just breasts)
1 1/2 cups olive oil
4 tablespoons freshly chopped garlic
1/2 teaspoon each dried: oregano, thyme, rosemary, and basil
1/2 teaspoon crushed red chili flakes
1/2 teaspoon salt
1/2 teaspoon freshly ground black pepper

Marinate the chicken in the oil and seasonings for 2 to 3 hours, or up to overnight.

For the roasted vegetable "carpaccio":
1 to 2 medium-sized, brightly-colored zucchinis
1 to 2 medium-sized, brightly-colored, yellow zucchinis
1 eggplant, long, slender, and firm
1 yellow sweet pepper
1 red sweet pepper
2 to 3 red tomatoes, a bit firm
Olive oil, as needed
Salt
Freshly ground black pepper

Preheat the oven to 250°F.

Slice the vegetables as thin as you are able. The peppers should be sliced vertically from top to bottom, discarding the seeds, stem, and white pith, into petals about 1/2-inch wide. (You'll get 6 to 8 petals per pepper.) The remaining vegetables should be sliced across into discs.

Lay the vegetables out on foil-line baking sheets. Drizzle them with olive oil, and season with salt and pepper. Roast in the oven until they begin to soften. This might take 20 minutes, or a bit more depending on how thinly they were sliced. You want them to soften and cook without much browning (they need to retain their color). Once the vegetables are cooked, allow them to rest at room temperature.

Meanwhile, remove the chicken from the marinade and grill or roast as you prefer. A crisp skin and deep, golden-brown exterior, and succulent, juicy, just-cooked-through interior are the goals.

On a large platter, preferably round, arrange the vegetables in concentric circles, matching colors and shapes. This whole dish relies on your artistic arrangement of the vegetables for its dramatic presentation value. Leave the center of the plate empty as a place to mound the chicken pieces. Once the chicken and vegetables are arranged, drizzle your best extra virgin olive oil over the platter, and scatter lightly with sea salt.

Chef's note: If you would like to add an additional element to the dish, sprinkle crumbled goat or feta cheese over the platter. But not too much, and be sure it's finely crumbled so you don't lose the colorful display.

northwest bison short ribs

from Wooldridge Creek Vineyard and Winery

WINE PAIRING
Wooldridge Creek
Vineyard & Winery
Merlot

What an interesting recipe this is: part French, part Mexican mole, and very Northwest with the bison. Chocolate and polenta are available through local providers on the internet (see our sources, page 183). Bison provides a great flavorful alternative to beef and is lower in fat, yet very delicious.

Serves 4 to 6

4 pound bone-in short ribs (Bison preferably, or substitute beef.)
1 tablespoon garlic salt
1 tablespoon Herbs de Provence
1 tablespoon freshly ground black pepper
1/2 cup olive oil
1/4 cup diced prosciutto
1 cup diced celery
1 cup diced carrots
3 cloves garlic, crushed
2 cups red wine
2 cups chicken stock
2 cups crushed canned tomatoes
3 sprigs fresh rosemary
6 sprigs fresh thyme
1 ounce Dagoba bittersweet chocolate
3 tablespoons unsalted butter
Finely chopped parsley, for garnish

Preheat the oven to 325°F.

Season the short ribs with the garlic salt, Herbs de Provence, and pepper. Heat the oil in a large, deep, ovenproof pan. Brown the short ribs well on all sides. Remove from the pan, and pour out the majority of the oil.

Add the prosciutto to the pan, and sauté for 1 minute. Add the celery, carrots, and garlic, and sauté for 5 to 8 minutes. Add the red wine, and reduce by half. Add the tomatoes, chicken broth, rosemary, and thyme. Cover, and bake for 4 hours, turning the meat over every hour.

Remove from the oven. Remove the ribs from the sauce. Strain the sauce, and skim off the fat.

When ready to serve, bring the sauce to a boil, and reduce by half, adding the chocolate and butter for the last five minutes. Add the short ribs to the sauce, and warm through. Serve over your favorite mashed potatoes or polenta. Garnish with the parsley.

oregon wine brotherhood

Created in 1929, the tradition of the Wine Brotherhood, originally established in the eleventh century was reestablished in France. The goals of the organization were to promote wine and the wine industry in general through educational and social efforts. In Oregon, the first brotherhood, then known as the Universal Order of the Knights of the Vines, was established by Dr. John Bauer in 1979. In 1994, the organization was renamed, and is now known as the Oregon Wine Brotherhood, and has been dedicated to the same goals and values as its ancient predecessors.

I have been honored to hold membership in the Brotherhood since 2001, and can attest to its dedicated support of Oregon's wine industry through education and scholarships that promote and expand interest and appreciation throughout the state, country, and the world. Our "unofficial" motto is: "We honor the grapes and the vines with respect and humility for the wines of Oregon!"

barbequed buffalo tri-tips

from Elk Cove Vineyards

At Elk Cove Vineyards, one of the most popular items is barbequed buffalo tri-tips.
They roast them hanging over a fire in a fifty-five-gallon drum, but they can easily be
prepared on a home gas grill although they won't be quite as smoked. The buffalo is
obtained just down the road from Elk Cove at L-Bar-T Bison Ranch.

Serves 4 to 6

1 (3-pound) buffalo tri-tip (approximate size)
4 green onions, chopped
4 cloves garlic, chopped
1 tablespoon freshly chopped ginger
1 teaspoon toasted sesame seeds
1 cup soy sauce
1 tablespoon sugar
3 tablespoons sesame oil

At least 6 hours or the night before, combine all the ingredients except the buffalo in a large glass dish or a resealable plastic bag. Add the buffalo tri-tip and refrigerate. Turn the buffalo occasionally so that all sides of the meat are exposed to marinade.

Preheat the grill to high heat (interior grill temperature should be 375°F).

Remove the buffalo from the marinade. Grill the tri-tip for 10 minutes, and then flip the meat to the other side. Grill for another 10 minutes, or until the internal temperature reaches 125°F. Watch the meat carefully the last few minutes for flare-ups and temperature. Remove the meat from the grill to a cutting board, cover it with foil, and allow it to rest for at least 5 to 10 minutes.

Thinly slice the meat on the diagonal against the grain. Serve immediately.

"Compromises are for relationships, not wine."

—SIR ROBERT SCOTT CAYWOOD

venison osso buco

from Dobbes Family Estate

Joe Dobbes shares this story: "I feel fortunate to have spent my boyhood days hunting and fishing with my father in the beautiful Oregon wilds. For me, food is a way to connect to the past. Every time I prepare this dish, I always think of those crisp fall mornings, in the moments before daybreak, tracking the path of a big buck. The aromas and flavors trigger memories so vivid that I am transported back in time and place. This is not a traditional osso bucco recipe, but a simplified version that allows the true, earthy flavors of the venison to come through. The recipe was inspired by John Manikowski's Wild Fish & Game Cookbook.

Serves 4

4 venison shanks
3 tablespoons canola oil
2 medium onions, finely chopped
8 cloves garlic, finely chopped
1 cup Pinot noir, or other dry, red wine
2 cups low-sodium homemade venison stock or one can beef stock
4 bay leaves
Kosher or sea salt
Freshly ground black pepper

Preheat the oven to 375°F.

Heat the oil in a large, cast iron skillet or Dutch oven over medium-high heat. Brown the venison shanks for approximately 5 minutes on all sides. Remove from the skillet. Add the onions and garlic to the remaining oil. Sauté until the onions become slightly translucent, but take care not to burn the garlic.

Add the wine (be sure to take a swig while you are at it). Deglaze the pan by taking a wooden spoon and scraping all of the good bits off of the bottom of the pan. Reduce the mixture by a third. This will take about 15 minutes. Add the remaining ingredients. Stir together well and return the venison back to the skillet, cover and roast for about 1 1/2 to 1 3/4 hours, or until the meat is tender. Remove the bay leaves. Serve one piece per person and be sure to pour a good amount of sauce over the meat.

WINE PAIRING
Eyrie Vineyards
2005 Estate Reserve
Pinot Noir

roast chicken

from Chef William King

This technique for roasting a chicken is something that everyone should be able to do well! A beautifully roasted chicken is one of the most soul-soothing meals known to man. Add seasonal vegetables or other accompaniments, and your menu is complete. The keys to success are a great, quality bird, the right seasoning, and the proper oven temperature. The results—perfection!

Serves 2

1 (approximately 2-pound) roasting chicken (Best-quality yields best results.)
2 to 3 tablespoon butter, very cold
2 to 3 teaspoons olive oil
1 to 2 tablespoons seasoning mixture
12 inches of kitchen twine

Seasoning mixture:
Equal parts:
Kosher salt
Freshly ground black pepper
Chopped rosemary, fresh or dried
Chopped thyme, fresh or dried
Chopped sage, fresh or rubbed

Place the oven rack in the center of the oven and preheat to 450°F.

Remove the giblet package. Rinse the bird, inside and out, and dry well.

Separate the skin from the bird by working your fingers under the skin over the breasts and thighs. Slice the butter into 6 to 8 pieces, and insert them under the skin. Three on each side of the breast bone, and 1 each on the thighs is ideal.

Rub olive oil over the entire bird, and sprinkle with the seasoning mixture.

The easiest method for trussing or tying a bird for the home cook to use is to bring the legs together, cross them at the ankles, and tie them together. If you start with plenty of twine (12 inches), it's easy and fast. Cut off any excess twine. Yes, there are more thorough ways to do this, but this technique will work just fine—the goal is to make the bird compact for consistent cooking.

Once the bird is trussed, place it in a roasting pan and roast for one hour.

Allow the chicken to rest for 15 minutes. Carve and serve with seasonal accompaniments *(see page 180)*. Always serve with pan juices.

Chef's note: Many instructions will tell you to poke the bird where the thigh and body meat come together, and if the juices run clear, the chicken is done. The problem with this technique is that the juices run out! You need the juice in the bird, not out in the pan. So, touch, look, timing, and experience all rule here. An average 3-pound chicken, roasted as described above, will be perfect in about 1 hour. You can baste the bird every 10 to 15 minutes, or not. I can argue both sides, so make it a personal preference. (I prefer to baste.)

seafood

White wine with fish is not an automatic choice. The key is to enjoy what you are drinking and eating. The Oregon Coast is blessed with as wide a range of seafood species as the recipes in this section well show. Don't be afraid to try something "red" with these preparations, you just might fall in love with the pairing.

bay scallop ceviche

from Trium

This is a wonderful luncheon or starter for dinner on a hot day. Served at "Tastes and Tapas" on the lawn for Trium, it is always a favorite. This is a great option for busy days since you prepare it well in advance.

Serves 4 as entrée or 12 as appetizer

1 1/2 pounds bay scallops
1/2 fresh sweet pineapple, peeled, cored, diced
1 mango, peeled, diced
1 papaya, peeled, diced
4 shallots, peeled, diced
1 bunch fresh cilantro, cleaned, chopped
1 jalapeño pepper, seeded, ribbed, small diced
1 1/2 cups freshly squeezed lime (or Meyer lemon juice)
Salt
Freshly ground black pepper
Sugar (optional)

Prepare the fruits, shallots, cilantro, and pepper and combine in a large, non-reactive bowl. Add the lime or lemon juice. Stir to coat well. Season to taste with the salt, pepper, and sugar.

Drain the scallops well, pat them dry, and add them to the fruit mixture. Stir well to mix. Refrigerate for a minimum of 4 hours, as the scallops in this recipe are raw, and are "cooked" by the citrus and fruit juices as they marinate.

Serve with chips, pita-bread quarters, or rustic bread.

cooking and pairing foods with wine

There is only one rule when it comes to the question of what to eat or pair with wines. The answer is: "Drink what you like!" If you have a favorite wine (or wines) and are comfortable with them, no matter what the specifics of the meal—*drink them!* Yes, there are guidelines that make sense and can improve the enjoyment of both food and wine when taken together: heavy, high-alcohol wines go well with full-flavored foods and softer wines with more delicate foods. Acid, oil, salt, and sugar all impact wine and acid and sugar are difficult to balance with wine. Salt, on the other hand, helps that balance when it comes to drinking reds. Spicy foods like spicy wines like zinfandel or maybe a syrah. The adage "whites with seafood, reds with meat" is generally true, but, I can drink a fabulous Oregon Pinot noir throughout a seven-course meal that includes both seafood and meats and be very happy! *Drink what you like!*

As for cooking with wine, the time-honored guidelines hold true. But again, there is one rule that should be adhered to under all circumstances, and that is: *only cook with wines that you would drink!* That's not to say that you need expensive, reserve wines to splash in a sauté, or add to a long, slow braise, but don't use bad wines (so, do they even make "cooking" wines any more? If so, *never* use them).

Throughout this book we have offered specific suggestions for Oregon wines to be paired with our recipes, and for wines to use as ingredients in the recipes themselves. We have done so to give you some direction and share our thoughts as to what might go best. But they are suggestions, albeit it educated ones. So, for one last time: *drink what you like!*

WINE PAIRING
Willakenzie Estate Winery
2006 Willamette Valley
Pinot Noir

salmon with pinot noir reduction

from Willakenzie Estate Winery

Chef Gilbert Henry offers the classic pairing of salmon and Pinot noir. The cream adds additional richness and "softens" the sauce while a small amount of lemon juice accentuates all the flavors. I recommend Oregon chinook salmon for this recipe, but any Northwest king or sockeye will work well.

Serves 4

4 (6-ounce) fillets of salmon
3 tablespoons butter
Salt
Freshly ground white pepper
1 cup fish broth
1 cup Willakenzie Pinot Noir
4 medium shallots, finely diced
1 cup heavy cream
1 tablespoon freshly squeezed lemon juice
Fresh parsley sprigs, for garnish

Preheat the oven to 350°F.

While 1 tablespoon of the butter is melting in a sauté pan, lightly season the fish with the salt and pepper. Place the salmon fillets top-side down in an ovenproof sauté pan so they do not touch each other. Lightly brown the salmon, then flip them over. Pour the fish broth, wine, and shallots over the fish. Bring to a slight boil and then transfer (in the same pan) to the oven for 5 to 10 minutes, depending on how you like your fish. (5 to 6 minutes for medium-rare.)

Place each fillet on a plate. Reduce the braising liquid over high heat. Add the cream, and reduce the mixture by half. Strain the sauce and whisk in the remaining 2 tablespoons of butter and the lemon juice. Pour the sauce over the salmon and garnish with a sprig of parsley. Serve with rice or steamed potatoes, and your choice of vegetables.

"It is better for pearls to pass through the lips of swine than good wine to pass through the lips of the indifferent"

—MARK LUEDTKE

WINE PAIRING
Adelsheim
2003 Chardonnay
Caitlin's Reserve

shrimp with risotto

from Chef William King

I make this dish often when Alaskan spot prawns are in season. The "spots" are a crustacean indigenous to the Pacific Northwest, and are sweet and firm. They pair beautifully with this risotto, and can be used as an appetizer, lunch, or dinner entrée, or if you are inclined towards extravagance as I am, as part of an elaborate Italian feast. Buon Appetito!

Serves 4 as a dinner entrée

24 spot prawns, peeled, deveined (or other large shrimp)
1 cup extra virgin olive oil
1/2 tablespoon crushed red chili flakes
1 teaspoon dried oregano
1 teaspoon dried thyme
Pinch salt
Pinch freshly ground black pepper

For the risotto:
8 cups chicken stock (or seafood stock)
1 teaspoon saffron, optional
1/4 cup olive oil
1 cup medium-diced onions
1 1/2 cups Arborio rice
1/4 cup white wine
4 tablespoons butter
1/3 cup grated Parmesan cheese

To prepare the risotto, heat the stock, and hold warm on the stove. If you choose to use the saffron, steep it in the stock for a few minutes.

Sauté the onions in the olive oil in a medium to large sauté pan until soft but not brown. Add the rice, and sauté to coat well with the oil. Brown the rice very slightly. Add about 1 cup of the stock and, stirring frequently, allow the rice to almost totally absorb the stock. Add another cup of stock and repeat the process.

Add the white wine with the final stock addition and reduce one final time. Remove from the heat and stir in the butter and Parmesan.

For the fresh tomato salsa:
Makes 2 cups

3 to 4 Roma tomatoes, small diced (about 1 cup)
3 tablespoons diced red onion
2 tablespoons freshly shredded basil leaves
2 to 3 tablespoons good-quality extra virgin olive oil
Pinch cracked black pepper
Big pinch good kosher or sea salt

Combine all the ingredients and blend well. Allow to sit for 1/2 hour or so before using.

To finish:
Marinate the prawns in the olive oil and seasonings and allow to rest for at least an hour or as long as overnight, refrigerated.

You may grill or sauté the shrimp. Either way, start with a very hot fire and cook briefly— they only take 3 to 4 minutes, and overcooked shrimp are a crime!

Spoon the risotto into serving bowls and top with the shrimp. Scatter the fresh tomato salsa over all, and serve immediately.

Chef's note: When they are in season, use colorful heirloom tomatoes in place of Romas for the tomato salsa.

barbecued oysters

from Brandborg Vineyard and Winery

Simple, but oh so good! Owner and winemaker Terry Brandborg was inspired to create this oyster presentation by restaurateur friends on Tomales Bay, near California's Point Reyes National Seashore.

Oysters (6 per person for an appetizer, more for an entrée)
1/2 pound butter, melted

Barbecue Sauce:
1 cup ketchup
Juice of 1 lemon
1 tablespoon horseradish
Tabasco® Pepper Sauce, to taste
Worcestershire sauce, to taste

Shuck the oysters, returning the meat to the half-shell. Discard the top shell. Place the oysters on the grill. Dollop them with butter (the grill will flame up). Close the lid, and wait a moment for the fire to settle down.

Open the lid, dollop the oysters with the barbecue sauce. Close the lid, and cook for 2 to 3 minutes. Serve hot.

¡Salud!

It is such an honor to live in a state and be part of an industry that does so much to give back to the community. There is perhaps no better example of taking care of your own than the organization *¡Salud!*, sponsor of the ¡Salud! Oregon Pinot Noir Auction.

¡Salud! was created by a group of Oregon winery owners and Tuality Healthcare physicians to address the hurdles faced by seasonal workers who cannot meet their basic health needs with only a few months' income that has to stretch over a full year. The vast majority of field workers move from one crop to another. Their temporary status with each employer makes them ineligible for health coverage. Without health insurance, these men and women and their families often do not seek professional healthcare until their problems become acute. Their knowledge of basic health education is poor and, they are overwhelmed by the maze of complex and confusing resources available in the medical system. *¡Salud!*'s mission is to fill this gap.

The relationship between vintners and physicians, united in their mission to benefit this essential workforce, is unique to Oregon. No other state in the country has such an effective and far-reaching program to support the seasonal-worker population. For more than fifteen years, the program has been supported solely by their Pinot noir auction. Held each November, the auction focuses on offering sought-after Pinot noirs created by Oregon's top wineries exclusively for this cause. In other ways, winery staff also assists medical professionals in accessing and educating workers and their families. This progressive approach by the Oregon wine industry has enabled *¡Salud!* to access workers at the work site as well as to identify those who are truly seasonal.

Our hats are off to this dedicated organization exemplifying the service to humanity that contributes to making Oregon such a unique and wonderful place to like and work!

harvest party halibut

from Ponzi Vineyards

Nancy Ponzi shares this story: "Several years ago, our dear family friends, Jules and Joan Drabkin, began a tradition that has become essential to our Harvest Party. In early summer, they retreat to their cabin on an island in Alaska's Inland Passage with the mission of catching enough halibut from the deep, cold water for the Ponzi Harvest Party.

Then, a huge cooler of marinating halibut fillets arrive at our annual Harvest Party. The Drabkins follow through with grilling and serving their exceptional entrée to the 100-plus harvesters (friends and family). We accompany the halibut with polenta—brought to perfect texture and taste in an enormous stainless-steel pan over an outside burner by polenta Diva, Monica Grinnell.

Marinara sauce, green salad, platters of sliced heirloom tomatoes, and Italian bread accompany the main feast with lots of wine for the adults and fresh-pressed Chardonnay juice for the kids. There's also an entire table full of showy desserts prepared by the harvesters."

Alaskan halibut, approximately 1/3 pound per person (thick fillets)

Marinade:
Mix in equal amounts:
   Olive oil
   Melted butter
Add in amounts to your taste:
   Lemon zest (lots!)
   Fresh thyme, parsley, tarragon, oregano
   Dried blended Herbs de Provence
   Pinot gris juice (Which you may not have, but perhaps use a bit of white grape juice.)
   Melted butter, for grilling

Prepare the marinade—be adventurous! The aroma alone will be inspiring. Marinate the halibut, covered, in the refrigerator for several hours, but no longer than twenty-four hours.

Oil the grill to prevent sticking.

The actual cooking time depends on the size of the fillets; grill approximately 4 to 5 minutes per side. The trick is to keep the fish moist as it quickly dries out…just brush or dribble on melted butter. A reliable test for doneness is to press the flesh with your finger: raw flesh is soft and springy, just right is barely firm, overdone is hard and firm.

Chef's note: Don't use acid—wine, vinegar, or lemon juice—for grilling this fish. It is incompatible with halibut.

grilled oregon steelhead
with caramelized pear beurre blanc

from Trium

Oregon steelhead and pears combine beautifully in this recipe, which is perfect for a spring run of these beautiful fish. Chef Ryan Gabel's suggestions for accompaniments are also ideal for a colorful spring dinner.

Serves 6

6 (4 to 6-ounce) Oregon steelhead fillets
4 pears (Bosc, Seckel, or Comice)
4 tablespoons brown sugar
2 cups Oregon Viognier
Juice from 1 Meyer lemon
1/2 pound chilled butter, small cubed
Salt
Freshly ground white pepper
Beurre blanc sauce *(page 178)*

Preheat the grill for the fish and the broiler for the pears.

Peel, core, and halve the pears. Place them in an ovenproof pan. Dust the tops with brown sugar. Broil to caramelize the sugar and partially cook the pears. Remove and set aside 1/2 pear per serving.

Use half of a pear for the sauce. Dice, and reserve.

Place the white wine and lemon juice in a non-reactive pan, and reduce to 1/4 cup. Remove the reduction from the heat and whisk in the cubed butter until incorporated. Add the diced pear and blend, using an immersion blender, until smooth. Add the salt and white pepper to taste. Hold the sauce by placing in a pan over warm (not hot) water while grilling the fish.

Season the steelhead with salt and pepper. Grill, cut-side down, briefly to make nice grill marks and carefully flip to the skin-side down to complete grilling.

Plate the grilled steelhead beside a caramelized pear half, and top with Beurre Blanc sauce.

Serve with asparagus, and Oregon wild mushrooms, and Jasmine rice seasoned with beet juice to add beautiful color contrast and flavors.

WINE PAIRING
Brandborg Vineyard
2006 Bench Lands
Pinot Noir

smoked salmon

from Brandborg Vineyard and Winery

This recipe is for the adventurous: we offer it because it exhibits the passion Oregon chefs, cooks, and winemakers have for preparing great food. This is a complicated process that requires time, attention, and more than a bit of experience. (But the results are terrific!)

Serves 6

6 smoked salmon fillets

Marinade:
2 cups brown sugar
2 cups white sugar
2 cups kosher salt
4 cups dark soy sauce
8 tablespoons finely minced garlic (1 whole large crown)
2 tablespoons cayenne pepper
1 tablespoon cinnamon
1 tablespoon nutmeg
1 tablespoon allspice

Combine all of the marinade ingredients in a non-reactive container, such as a large stainless-steel pot. Mix well until the sugar and salt dissolve in the soy sauce. Marinate the salmon overnight for up to 12 hours, but no longer, or the fish will get too salty.

Remove the salmon fillets from the marinade, pat them dry, and place them on racks while the fire gets going.

Place the fillets, skin-side down, on parchment paper on top of aluminum foil, and then trim them to the size of the fillet. Smoke in a water-smoker until done. (I use a New Braunfels chimney tower type with a side wood box.)

The fuel is the key. Start the fire with Lazzari mesquite charcoal, and add very small, stove-sized pieces of split alder (more charcoal may be used if needed, for more heat). Smoke time will vary greatly depending on the heat of your fire, and the rack the fillets are on (closer to the fire, or higher in the chimney). Smoke the fillets until a meat thermometer reaches 135°F to 140°F degrees, and the salmon is firm, but not hard to the touch. Minimum time is usually about 3 hours, and maximum time is 6 to 8 hours. Keep the fish moist, and be careful not to overcook!

Serve on a very good sourdough baguette or crostini. At Brandborg, we use a traditional Swedish whole rye crisp bread called Knäckebröd. Smoked salmon is also excellent in omelets with feta cheese, chervil, and chives or green onions.

pepper-crusted tuna steaks

from Sokol Blosser Winery

Simple, healthful and delicious, I love this preparation. With no fancy sauces, its success depends on the quality of the ingredients. Make sure that the fish is fresh and bright-looking and has uniform thickness. In the Northwest, go local with albacore tuna. Allow about one-third of a pound per person. Grilled tuna and Pinot noir are so wonderful together, this meal feels like a celebration!

Serves 4

4 (3/4 to 1-inch thick) albacore tuna steaks
Coarsely ground black pepper (or try a mix of black, rose, and green pepper)
2 tablespoons extra virgin olive oil

Completely coat the steaks with the pepper. Heat the olive oil in a sauté pan to very hot. Sear the steaks on all sides. The object is to create a nice crust on the outside and warm the interior, but leave it virtually uncooked. The outside will be firm, even crunchy, and the inside will melt in your mouth. The entire cooking time should be about 3 to 4 minutes, about a minute each on the top and bottom, and about 20 seconds each on the sides and ends.

Plate immediately. Serve with one of Lundberg Farms' organic rice mixtures, a fresh seasonal green vegetable, and Sokol Blosser Pinot Noir.

the chef and the vintner

It is hard to imagine a better environment in which to work as a chef or as a winemaker than that of our magnificent state of Oregon, and more specifically, the Willamette Valley. Yes, in a weak moment you might get me to acknowledge that California's Napa Valley is a strong rival, its viticulture certainly more heralded. But consider the highlights of our region's indigenous products: First are certainly our wine grapes, producing numerous award-winning varietals with arguably the finest Pinot grapes in the world. The vintners are blessed with soil and climate that allow them to work their magic in one of the most beautiful areas of the country.

And then there are the agricultural products and those from Oregon's waters, forests, farms and ranches that provide chefs with foodstuffs of unparalleled variety and quality. Tree fruit, cane berries, asparagus, mint, wheat, lamb, beef—organically raised and wonderful to cook. Dungeness crab, bay shrimp, coastal fish, oysters, steelhead, and the king of fish, Wild Pacific and Columbia River salmon are all abundant and sustainable and the best in the world. These are the gifts of our region. These are the products we enjoy throughout the year that have inspired and supported a new generation of chefs who have made the use of local ingredients a standard and a model for other areas of the country.

Together, vintners and chefs have established our state as a leader in all things "of the table." Together, we have brought the celebration of great wines and foods into the daily regional and national dialogue. Together, we have confirmed the relationship that winemakers and chefs can create and enjoy the magnificent benefits of that effort. A meal "at the Oregon Table" is a meal complete. A balance of seafoods and meats, of delicate and bold flavors. From our hors d'oeuvre of Columbia River Chinook Salmon Tartare, to a velvety Cream of Canby Asparagus Soup, or to a Hazelnut Crusted Lamb Loin balanced by a deep Pinot noir reduction, then artisan cheeses from Rogue Creamery, with a finish of Willamette Valley Blackberry-Raspberry short cake with buttermilk biscuits. The foods are exquisite. Then the pairings…perhaps a Sokol Blosser Pinot gris…Adelsheim's Caitlin's Reserve Chardonnay…then a Pinot. How can you choose? Domaine Serene, Ponzi, Archery Summit, Arcus—or a dozen others! Even the cheeses and desserts find partners with Oregon's emerging ports. This is a meal to remember—celebrating who we are and where we are from. This is a meal at the Oregon Table and a testimonial to the value of partnership. The partnership between the chef and the vintner. *Salud!*

northwest cedar-planked steelhead trout

from Willamette Valley Vineyards

Cedar-roasting is as traditional a cooking method as exists in the Pacific Northwest, dating back hundreds of years to Native Americans who cooked salmon on cedar skewers and planks around campfires. Now Jim Bernau, founder of Willamette Valley Vineyards, gives us this recipe, adapted for steelhead and today's backyard barbecues.

Serves 3 to 4

1 (1 to 1 1/2-pound) steelhead trout fillet, skin on, pin bones removed
1 untreated (1/2 by 6 by 18-inches) cedar plank, for grilling
1/4 cup olive oil
1 large lemon, juiced
Sea salt
Freshly ground white pepper
Freshly chopped parsley, for garnish
Lemon, for garnish

Soak the cedar plank in water for two hours or more.

Rinse the fish with cold water and pat dry with paper towel. Place the steelhead fillet, skin-side-down on the cedar plank.

Combine the olive oil and lemon juice in a small bowl. Brush the top of the fish with the mixture. Sprinkle with sea salt and freshly ground white pepper. Reserve at room temperature.

Heat the grill to 400°F to 425°F. Use indirect heat if using a charcoal grill.

When the grill or coals are hot, place the cedar plank with the steelhead fillet on the grill. Close the lid and cook for 15 to 20 minutes, allowing the cedar smoke to infuse the steelhead. Carefully lift the lid, the outside of the steelhead should be opaque while the center is still translucent. Cook a few minutes longer if you prefer the fillet opaque throughout. The steelhead should slide easily off the skin and cedar plank for serving.

Garnish with chopped parsley and lemon. Serve with a fresh green salad and wild rice.

halibut with porcini-ginger sauce

from Joel Palmer House

This terrific recipe from Chef Chris Czarnecki provides an Asian spin on one of the Pacific Northwest's most prized seafood species—halibut. The sauce/glaze is complex and delicious, and keeps the fish very moist. Trust me, this one is addictive. Feel free to try the preparation with other fish, or even chicken.

Serves 4

4 (8-ounce) halibut fillets
1 quart water (or 1 quart porcini stock)
4 ounces dried porcini (Omit if using porcini stock.)
3/4 cup soy sauce
1/4 cup white wine vinegar
1 tablespoon sliced jalapeño (optional)
1 tablespoon sesame oil
1 teaspoon salt
1 cup sliced onion
1 teaspoon dried or fresh basil
1/2 teaspoon freshly ground black pepper
1/2 cup sugar
1/4 cup plum wine
1/4 cup cornstarch
1/4 cup water
1/2 cup pickled ginger
1/2 cup freshly chopped cilantro
1/2 cup sliced green onion

For the rice:
2 cups rice
4 cups water
1 tablespoon salt
2 tablespoon Nori Komi Furikake (prepared sesame seed and seaweed)

Preheat the oven to 450°F.

To prepare the rice, combine the rice, water, salt, and Nori Komi Furikake. Simmer until the rice is cooked, and the water has evaporated.

Combine the water, porcini, soy sauce, vinegar, jalapeño, sesame oil, salt, onion, basil, pepper, sugar, and plum wine into a pot and bring to boil. Simmer for 5 minutes.

Stir the cornstarch and water together in separate container. Add to the pot, while stirring, and briefly bring the pot to boil. Add the ginger, and simmer for an additional 5 minutes. Strain the sauce through fine sieve.

Cover the halibut with enough sauce to coat, and reserve the rest. Bake in the oven for 5 minutes or until cooked through.

Combine the cilantro and green onion, and add to the remaining sauce just before serving.

To serve, create a bed of rice on 4 serving plates, and place a halibut fillet on each. Cover the halibut in the sauce, cilantro, and green-onion mixture. The sauce can be refrigerated for up to a week.

Chef's note: You will have extra sauce. This recipe makes 1 1/2 quarts, which serves up to 10.

pasta & vegetarian

Some of these pasta recipes contain meat and/or seafood. Some do not. The vegetarian recipes are meatless, but may not satisfy a vegan's needs. What you can be sure of is that each of these preparations is delicious and showcases our regional bounty very well!

lamb ragu
with penne and fresh ricotta

from Chef William King

This is a rich and satisfying dish that soothes the soul on a dark, winter night. It stands alone as a terrific pasta entrée, a hearty appetizer, or even an early course in a lavish multi-course Italian meal. However you serve it, the star of this meal is Anderson Ranch Lamb. Dave Anderson is a pioneer in naturally raised lamb and his hard work and commitment show in the outstanding quality of his meat.

Serves 8 as an appetizer, or 6 entrées, with plenty of leftovers.

2 pounds lamb shoulder, 1/2-inch dice
4 tablespoons vegetable oil
1 tablespoon Montreal seasoning
1/2 tablespoon dried thyme
1/2 tablespoon finely chopped dried rosemary
1/2 tablespoon cumin
6 to 8 quarts water
3 tablespoons salt
1 pound penne or ziti pasta
1/2 cup fresh ricotta cheese, for garnish
¼ cup grated Parmesan cheese, for garnish

For the sauce:
1 bottle leftover cabernet and/or pinot from the other night (Use a good drinking wine.)
3 tablespoons oil
1 cup medium-dice yellow onion
1/2 cup medium-dice carrot
1/2 cup medium-dice celery
3 tablespoons chopped garlic
3 cups tomato sauce
3 tablespoons tomato paste
1/2 cup sherry
1 cup water
1 tablespoon crushed red chili flakes

To prepare the lamb, heat a large sauté pan, 14 to 16 inches if available, to very hot. Add the oil and heat to the smoking point. Add the lamb and arrange in a single layer over the surface of the pan. Don't be tempted to turn or stir the meat, as it needs to cook and brown undisturbed for 8 to 10 minutes, or until very well browned. Add the seasonings, stir the meat and allow it to cook in its own juices for another 5 minutes. Meanwhile, bring 6 to 8 quarts of water to a boil in a large sauce pot to cook the pasta. Add 3 tablespoons of salt.

While this is working, prepare the sauce. Bring the wine to a boil in a sauce pan and reduce to about 1 1/2 cups and reserve. Heat the oil in a medium to large saucepot. Add the vegetables and sauté to soften. Add the reserved wine reduction, tomato sauce, paste, sherry, water, and chili flakes, and bring to a boil, then lower to a simmer. When the meat is ready, add it and the pan juices to the tomato sauce. Simmer for about 30 to 40 minutes, or until the lamb is tender and the sauce is thickened.

Add the penne to the boiling water and cook according to package instructions. Drain well and divide onto serving plates or bowls. Ladle generous amounts of the lamb ragu over the penne. With a standard teaspoon (not a measuring spoon, the kind of spoon you'd use to stir coffee) arrange dollops of the ricotta over the ragu. Sprinkle with the Parmesan cheese and serve.

risotto with portobellos and peas

from Viento Wines

If you leave out the Parmigiano-Reggiano and substitute vegetable stock in this flavorful dish, you'll have vegetarian, even vegan risotto. When winemaker Rich Cushman and his family dine together, they prepare the vegan version. The stirring and slow addition of the stock are critical to making a great, creamy risotto.

Serves 4 to 6

1/4 cup finely diced onion
3 tablespoons extra virgin olive oil
1 cup Arborio rice
1/2 cup aromatic dry white wine (Viento Viognier or Verona)
3 to 4 cups chicken stock (or vegetable stock)
1 cup frozen petite peas
2 medium portobello mushrooms
1 tablespoon balsamic vinegar
1/2 cup freshly grated Parmigiano-Reggiano cheese
Salt
Freshly ground black pepper

Sauté the onion in 1 tablespoon of olive oil in a Dutch oven over medium heat until soft and translucent, about 5 minutes. Add the rice, heat through, and coat with oil. Add the wine to the pan, and allow the rice to "toast" in the oil for a few minutes.

Stirring regularly, add the stock, 1/2 cup at a time—adding more as the stock is absorbed— until the rice has an al dente, yet creamy texture. This will take about 25 to 30 minutes. Add the green peas for the last few minutes of cooking.

While preparing the risotto, dice the portobello stems and one cap to medium dice. Slice the remaining caps 1/2-inch wide. Sauté in olive oil, and finish with 1 tablespoon of balsamic vinegar.

Stir the mushrooms into the finished risotto. Add the cheese, unless preparing a vegan dish. Season to taste with salt, and serve topped with freshly ground black pepper.

a unique cellaring program

As interest and enthusiasm for the Oregon wine industry grows, it is becoming increasingly difficult for restaurants to feature older vintage wines. Wineries like to bottle their wines and release them as quickly as possible and, in turn, restaurants and wine shops want to rapidly move the product from their shelves. Often the only place you can find older wines is in personal cellars.

The University Club in Portland, Oregon has created a unique, ongoing cellaring program. Their wine specialists have identified the most important varietals to have available for their members and have set aside a significant amount of their wine budget to purchase high-quality, long-lasting wines. Once purchased, these wines are then "cellared" for a minimum of five to ten years after their release before they appear on the Club's wine list. This allows them to offer older vintages, as well as creating exciting vertical opportunities within individual types and varieties. For instance, with one label, they offer "verticals" from 1992 to 2003, allowing them to have both broad variety and great depth within any wine category... of course, patience is required, *and* self-discipline.

fresh tomato pasta
and filetto piccolo

from Ponzi Vineyards

The combination of summer, recent memories of meals in Italy and a silky, luxurious Pinot noir is the inspiration for Nancy Ponzi's suggested simple dinner. One warm evening here in the Willamette Valley, the Ponzi family's good friend and houseguest, Luca Currado of Cantina Vietti in Piemonte, went to the garden and gathered a large handful of basil and a bowl of cherry tomatoes. His revelation "recipe" of tomato sauce follows. His appreciation and respect for pure taste, and for food products in their natural glory, is not unusual in Italy. In fact, it's normal, expected, and fundamental. Food is grown with care, prepared with care, presented in its natural beauty and consumed with attention and joy.

Serves 4 to 6

Fresh Tomato Pasta:
4 cups perfectly ripe, diced cherry tomatoes
2 large cloves garlic, finely chopped
1 cup freshly chopped basil
1 tablespoon medium/coarse salt
2 tablespoons coarse salt, for pasta water
12 to 16 ounces cappellini pasta of excellent quality
4 tablespoons fine-quality olive oil
1 cup finely grated Parmigiano-Reggiano cheese
Basil, for garnish

Place the tomatoes, garlic, basil and salt into a colander placed over a sink. Mix gently, then leave for at least a half an hour to drain and marry the flavors.

Boil a large pot of salted water for cooking pasta. Boil the pasta just until tender and drain, shaking the colander to remove all of the cooking water.

Place the pasta into a mixing bowl. Toss with olive oil. Toss with the drained tomato mixture. Add the Parmigiano-Reggiano. Toss well. Add more salt if needed.

Serve in individual bowls garnished with fresh basil. Accompany at the table with bowls of Parmigiano-Reggiano, extra olive oil, salt, bread and, of course, the Ponzi Pinot Noir.

Filetto Piccolo:
1 small fillet (3/4 to 1-inch thick) per person
Olive oil
Kosher salt
Freshly ground black pepper
Approximately 1/2 cup Pinot noir

Salt and pepper the fillets. Heat the olive oil in a heavy, very flat-bottomed sauté pan. When very hot, add the fillets. Cook for 4 minutes on each side for medium rare. Remove the fillets to serving platter.

To deglaze, add the wine to the sauté pan. Reduce the heat a little, but maintain a boil. Stir to integrate the residue from the pan until the wine reduces to a saucy texture. Pour over the fillets.

Serve with a garden salad—just greens, vinegar, olive oil and salt, and country-style Italian bread (no sourdough). And the wine…well, the Ponzi Pinot Noir will bring every aspect together and the last glasses can be dessert!

Chef's note: If you have access to organic tenderloin, it's worth the expense. I buy full tenderloin and cut the steaks as needed. The meat is of such high quality it will keep for a long time, especially wrapped in vacuum packs.

WINE PAIRING
Bethel Heights
2004 Pinot Gris

capellini with manila clams

from Chef William King

Here's my take on the classic Italian pasta with white clam sauce. This version is loaded with garlic and herb flavor, and features the beautifully buttery steamer clams from the Pacific Northwest.

Serves 4

3 dozen manila clams
8 ounces shucked manila clams (or chopped canned clams)
3/4 pound capellini, angel hair or thin spaghetti
3 tablespoons sliced garlic
1 tablespoon chopped shallots
2 tablespoons extra virgin olive oil
4 tablespoons butter
1/2 cup heavy cream
1/2 teaspoon dried thyme (or fresh if available)
1/2 teaspoon dried oregano (or fresh if available)
1 teaspoon crushed red chili
1 teaspoon kosher salt
1/4 cup sherry
4 tablespoons julienned peppadew peppers, for garnish

Cook the pasta to the al dente stage in plenty of heavily salted boiling water.

While the pasta is cooking, sauté the shucked clams, garlic, and shallots in the olive oil and butter in a large sauté pan. Add the cream and seasonings. Add the sherry and the manila clams in the shell. Cover the pan for 1 to 2 minutes, or until the clams are open.

Drain the pasta and immediately add to the pan.

Toss well, and arrange in bowls. Garnish with the julienned peppers.

the classic wines auction

In 1982, a small group of friends came together to auction exceptional Oregon wines and donate the proceeds to Portland-based charities. They raised about $9,000. Today, the Classic Wines Auction is one of the top-ten largest wine-based charity events in the country, its most recent annual effort raised $2.8 million. The Classic Wines Auction is an extravagant event with extravagant goals and results in magnificent outreach to those in need—children and families throughout the greater Portland metropolitan area. Generously supported by winemakers and chefs, the Classic Wines Auction is yet another representation of the type of dedication to community that Oregon's wine industry and restaurants provide.

truffled tofu
with spring vegetables

from Lange Estate Winery and Vineyards

Here is an interesting recipe from Lange Estate Winery and Vineyard that treats tofu like veal or chicken cutlets. Tofu and truffles? Don't knock it 'til you try it.

Serves 6

2 (1-pound) packages extra-firm tofu
2 tablespoons truffle salt
1 pound mushrooms
2 leeks
1 pound asparagus
4 cups arugula
1 pound parpadelle pasta
Olive oil
2 cups vegetable or chicken stock
1 teaspoon truffle oil
1 shallot, minced
4 tablespoons butter
Sea salt
Freshly cracked pepper
Freshly sliced Asiago cheese

Rinse and pat the tofu dry, slice into cutlets and arrange on a dish or platter. Sprinkle the truffle salt on the cutlets, thoroughly covering both sides. Let sit for at least one hour. (This can be done a day ahead and refrigerated.)

Clean the mushrooms and leeks. Slice the mushrooms for sautéing, and cut the leeks lengthwise, discarding the toughest parts. Rinse and trim the asparagus. Rinse the arugula, and trim away the stalks. Fill a pot with salted water for cooking the parpadelle. Pour yourself a glass of Lange Chardonnay, sip, enjoy!

Heat the olive oil in an iron or nonstick skillet. Sear the tofu cutlets on both sides, being mindful to get a good, crusty seal on each side. You may need to do this in batches, or you can have two pans going at once. After the cutlets have been seared, slowly add the stock and the truffle oil to the pan. Cover, and poach the cutlets for 8 to 10 minutes. Remove the cutlets, cover and set aside, keeping them hot.

Add the remaining stock, the shallot, mushrooms and 2 teaspoons of butter, and reduce to make a quick pan jus to pour over the cutlets. Cook the pasta according to the package directions. Rinse and drain. Sauté the leeks and asparagus in butter and olive oil. Season to taste with salt and pepper. When the vegetables are done, add the arugula to the pan, just to wilt.

Gently toss the vegetables and pasta together. Divide equally among warm plates. Arrange the tofu cutlets alongside, pour pan jus over the top, garnish with sliced Asiago cheese, and serve. Share the remaining Lange Chardonnay with your dinner companions!

lemon fettucini

with smoked salmon, dill, and vodka cream sauce

from Chateaulin Restaurant Français

Popular recipes for pasta with vodka cream sauce have traveled the road from inventive to classic and beyond. This refreshing variation from Chef David Taub with the lemon pasta and smoky salmon just might become a favorite in your kitchen.

Serves 4

12 ounces cold-smoked salmon lox, julienne
1 (8.8-ounce) package Rusticella Lemon Fettucini, cooked al dente (See chef's note.)
3 cups heavy cream
1/2 cup vodka
1/2 medium red onion, diced
2 tablespoons lightly chopped fresh dill
2 tablespoons lightly chopped fresh chervil
2 tablespoons ground rose peppercorns
Sea salt
4 teaspoons whitefish caviar, for garnish

Bring the cream, vodka, and red onion to a boil using a large, non-reactive sauté pan, and reduce by half. Add half of the fresh herbs, and half of the rose pepper. Add the salmon and the pasta. Stir well, and cook over medium heat until slightly thickened. Add salt as needed before dividing onto four plates. Garnish each plate with the remaining herbs, rose pepper, and a teaspoon of caviar.

Chef's note: You can substitute regular fettucini cooked and tossed with 1 tablespoon of minced lemon zest for the Rusticella fettucini.

---

some thoughts on service

Of all the aspects of at-home wine service, holding and serving the wine at the proper temperature and giving the wine a bit (or sometimes a lot) of aeration or oxidation are the two most important things to remember. Often, wines are served at the wrong temperature—even in restaurants—reds tend to be too warm, and whites too cold. Room temperature—most typically 69 to 72°F is not the correct temperature for red wine. I recommend 60 to 65°F, depending on the varietal, with Oregon Pinot noir drinking extremely well at about the middle of that range. For whites, the 40°F temperature of your refrigerator is too cold, my preference being more toward 45 to 50°F. Like most things about wine, these are personal preferences. I will always be in favor of drinking wines in the fashion that makes you happy. But temperature matters, so keep that in mind.

Now, as far as aeration or oxidation, as we have heard, wine is literally a living, breathing substance, and, as a result, it needs a little air. Opening a bottle and allowing it to sit unpoured does not quite get the job done—there is not enough surface area, and exposure is limited. The solution is simple, yet is usually ignored: Decant the wine! You do not need the overly fancy approach, reserved for old reds that usually have sediment that needs to be avoided. A fancy crystal decanter is not required either. Keep it simple, easy, and fun. Just pour the wine into a huge pitcher, from about 4 to 5 inches above its mouth, and your wine will receive a perfect breath of fresh air. That's it! And yes, I recommend this simple ritual for almost all reds, as long as there is no concern about sediment. Proper temperature and adequate air are pretty basic steps, yet are very effective and will greatly enhance your enjoyment!

WINE PAIRING
Domaine Drouhin Oregon
2005 Pinot Noir Laurène

wild mushroom pot pie
with sharp cheddar pastry

from Chef William King

Spring and fall each bring their own array of wild mushrooms to the Pacific Northwest. Morels, chanterelles, cèpes, black trumpets. At market prices these treasures can raise the cost of a homestyle pot pie to forty dollars or more. Making this with a mixture of domestic button mushrooms and their wild cousins will help keep the cost down. You can decide what does or doesn't break the bank. Either way, this is a rich, delicious vegetarian option that makes a great lunch or dinner entrée. The Cheddar cheese is an added bonus of flavor and richness.

Serves 4 (makes 2 pot pies in 8 by 2-inch deep casseroles)

For the crust:

1 2/3 cups flour
1/4 teaspoon salt
1/2 cup plus 2 tablespoons butter, small cubes

2 ounces grated sharp or extra-sharp Cheddar cheese
2 tablespoons cold water
2 large egg yolks

Combine the flour, salt, butter and Cheddar and blend until the mixture resembles coarse meal. Mix the water and egg yolks, and add to the flour mixture. Gather the dough and form into two balls, being careful not to overwork the dough. Form the dough into two 6-inch discs. Wrap the discs in plastic wrap and refrigerate for at least one hour.

For the filling:

1 cup medium-dice onion
1 cup medium-dice carrot
1 cup medium-dice celery
4 tablespoons butter, divided
1 pound button mushrooms, quartered or large slices
3/4 pound seasonal wild mushrooms, sliced or roughly chopped
2 tablespoons oil
4 tablespoons all-purpose flour

3/4 cup vegetable stock or broth
1/2 cup sherry
1 cup heavy cream
1/8 teaspoon dried thyme
1/8 teaspoon salt
1/8 teaspoon freshly ground black pepper
2 tablespoons chopped parsley

Preheat the oven to 400°F.

Sauté the onion, carrot, and celery in 2 tablespoons of butter, until somewhat soft and lightly brown. Reserve. Sauté the mushrooms in 2 tablespoons of butter and oil until they are well browned. Add the reserved vegetables back into the pan with the mushrooms. Blend in the flour. Cook for 3 to 4 minutes. Add the stock, sherry, and cream. Blend thoroughly, and simmer to reduce until fairly thickened. Add the seasoning and parsley and allow to cool for a few minutes.

To assemble: Roll the pastry dough out to form 2 (10-inch) crusts. Fill 2 (8 by 2-inch) casserole dishes with the filling. Top with the pastry crusts and crimp the edges. Bake until the crust is golden brown, about 20 to 25 minutes. Allow to cool for a couple of minutes before serving.

WINE PAIRING
Viento Wines
Sangiovese or Verona

caramelized onion and feta pizza

from Viento Wines

Want to try your hand at homemade pizza? Here's a nice, simple version from owner and winemaker Rich Cushman at Viento Wines. Anchovies, as is often the case, are optional, but the caramelized onions, balsamic, and feta have plenty of flavor on their own.

Makes 1 pizza

Topping:
3 large onions, thinly sliced
1 tablespoon butter
1 tablespoon olive oil
1/4 cup white wine
1 tablespoon balsamic vinegar
Cornmeal, for preparing the pan
1 scant cup crumbled feta cheese
Anchovies (optional)
Salt
Freshly ground black pepper

Pizza dough:
1 tablespoon yeast
1 cup water
3 cups all-purpose flour
1 tablespoon olive oil
1 teaspoon salt

Start by making the pizza dough in the morning, or 3 to 4 hours in advance.

Suspend 1 tablespoon of yeast in 1 cup of warm water, and let stand for 5 minutes, or until the yeast is bubbly and showing activity. Add 1 cup of flour and mix gently. Let stand for 10 minutes. Add 1 tablespoon of olive oil and 1 teaspoon salt, and mix. Mix in the remaining flour, knead until smooth. Coat the dough with olive oil and let it rise in a covered bowl until it has at least doubled in bulk. Punch down the dough, and let rise again.

Preheat the oven to 500°F.

To caramelize the onions, sauté on low to medium heat in 1 tablespoon of butter and 1 tablespoon of olive oil, until soft and just browning, about 20 to 30 minutes. Add 1/4 cup dry white wine (Viento Verona or Riesling work great). Simmer for 5 minutes or more, and then add 1 tablespoon of good-quality balsamic vinegar.

To assemble: Roll out the pizza dough so it is very thin. Sprinkle the cornmeal on the pizza pan, and place the dough on the pan. Top the dough with caramelized onions. Crumble the feta over the onions. Add anchovies and salt, as desired. Grind fresh black pepper lightly over the top.

Bake in the oven on a preheated pizza stone for 10 minutes.

Slice, serve, and enjoy.

"Both to rich and poor, wine is the happy antidote for sorrow."

—EURIPIDES

spaghettini
with brie and pan-roasted tomatoes

from Chef William King

Very light yet rich in flavor, this is a great summer supper. The key is serving the pasta at just the right temperature so that the brie is soft and melting, but not liquefied. A nice green salad and some crusty bread, and this dinner can be on your table in twenty minutes.

Serves 2

16 to 20 ounces cooked spaghettini (Whatever you like for 2 helpings.)
3 tablespoons extra virgin olive oil
About 20 cherry tomatoes, left whole
3 tablespoons freshly chopped basil
4 ounces brie, 1-inch dice, "rind" left on
1/2 tablespoon cracked black pepper
Pinch salt
3 to 4 tablespoons freshly grated Parmesan cheese

Cook, drain and rinse the pasta, and measure out two portions. The pasta should be just a little wet as the water will help keep the pasta moist in the pan. Reserve.

Heat the olive oil in a large sauté pan, add the tomatoes and let them brown for about 1 1/2 minutes. Shake the pan, and add the pasta and basil. Toss well to heat the pasta thoroughly.

Remove the pan from the heat, and add the brie. Season to taste with salt and pepper. Toss very well until the brie and tomatoes are evenly distributed and the brie is clearly starting to soften and melt, about 2 minutes.

Grate the Parmesan over the pasta, and serve immediately.

respect and protect

Oregon's wine industry has successfully evolved by maintaining a high level of respect for quality and for individualism. Yet no greater level of respect is attributed to the efforts of vineyard and winery owners than that of respect for, and protection of, our magnificent environment. Though much has been made of the image of Oregon's wine pioneers as iconoclastic and individualists, in truth it is their commitment to community and collaboration that has established this region as a leader in the industry in practices related to ecology and sustainability through membership in, and support of, organizations such as Low Input Viticulture & Ecology, Inc. (Live) a non-profit organization dedicated to maintain the highest standards of sustainable viticulture practices, Leadership in Energy and Environment Design (LEED®), Green Building Rating System™, which sets the standards for sustainable building construction, and Salmon-Safe, which helps vineyards protect and restore salmon habitat through a variety of sustainable agricultural methods. Oregon's winemakers lead the world in their commitment to environmental protection.

dessert

Pairing wine with dessert can be tricky. There are wonderful dessert wines from all over the world and Oregon's repertoire is varied and impressive. But many people don't go for these sweet, rich complements to desserts. For me it's easy, I go back to my most basic rule: drink what you like. Just so you understand that sugar and "dry" wines are natural enemies, feel free to enjoy your Pinot noir or chardonnay all the way through the sweet course.

cheese service

from Chef William King

WINE PAIRING
Try a flight of three of
your favorite Pinot noirs
or ports

Selecting cheese is a personal process, depending upon your taste preferences. Cheese textures vary from soft to firm, with flavors that range from mild to blue, and even "stinky." We're very fortunate to have a superb variety of styles here in the Pacific Northwest. Whatever your selection, it is important to allow the cheeses to warm to room temperature before serving. This allows the aroma and flavors to fully develop.

Presenting an array of cheeses makes for the most interesting experience. As for wine pairings, different cheeses may suggest different wines, but most cheeses are wine-friendly due to their fairly high salt content, which is desirable when pairing food with wine. If you choose a limited wine selection with your cheese, try to include a good Pinot noir. This signature varietal from Oregon is perhaps the most versatile in pairing with both mild and more assertive cheeses. I like a selection of five to six cheeses—a blue, a double or triple crème, a goat, something firm and perhaps a Cheddar—providing choices with all of your guests in mind. Fresh or dried fruit add texture, balance, and roasted nuts provide a bit more salt. All you need is some crusty baguette slices and you have an hors d'oeuvre, a post-meal finale, a dessert replacement or supplement, or even a full meal.

Pictured are a Farmstead Smoked Gouda, French Prairie Brie (both from Willamette Valley Cheese Company), and Rogue Creamery Oregonzola, Tumalo Farms "Capricorn," all from Oregon, and a French-washed rind.

the oregon—burgundy connection

It is not by chance that Oregon's most highly regarded wines are Pinot noirs. The pioneers of Oregon's wine industry did their homework and, although many different varietals were planted in those early years, it was the great grape of Burgundy that dominated their focus and has produced "Best-in-the-World" awards over the years.

It is certainly not that the Pinot noir is the easiest grape to grow, to the contrary, Pinot noir is a fragile, often uncooperative vine from which to nurture and produce wine. But, as with most agricultural products, and even more true of wine grapes, you grow what the land, the soil, and the climate allow. In Oregon, all of these environmental factors are remarkably similar to those of the Burgundy region of France, where the Pinot noir grape is King and is the foundation of some of the greatest wines in history. The Oregon path was quite clear: Grow Pinot!

The heart of Oregon's primary wine-growing area, like that of Burgundy, straddles the Earth's forty-fifth parallel. Its cool climate and unique blend of volcanic and sedimentary soils combine to create a growing environment that is remarkably similar to that of the French-growing region. The results are unique in subtle ways and are, of course a function of wine making as well, but the Oregon-Burgundy connection is unquestionable, with clone vines now producing some of the world's finest wines in Oregon, as original "Mother" vines have for centuries in Burgundy. Vive La France! *Vive Le Oregon!*

rustic pear tart

with late harvest viognier syrup and crème fraîche

from RoxyAnn Winery

I love pears, and the rich, fruity sweetness of a late-harvest Viognier beautifully complements the natural sugars in roasted pears. This free-form tart from RoxyAnn Winery is delicious with its pear flavor and wine syrup. The dollop of crème fraîche completes and balances with creamy tartness.

Serves 8

Crust:
1 1/2 cups all-purpose flour
3 tablespoons sugar
1/2 teaspoon salt
10 tablespoons (1 1/4 stick) chilled, unsalted butter, cut into pieces
1 large egg yolk
1 tablespoon late-harvest Riesling (or other sweet white dessert wine)

Filling:
3 large ripe, but firm Comice pears, peeled, cored, thinly sliced
1 tablespoon sugar
1 tablespoon all-purpose flour

Late-Harvest Viognier Syrup:
1 cup, plus 2 tablespoons late-harvest Viognier (or other sweet white dessert wine)
1/2 cup water
1/2 cup sugar

Crème fraîche, for garnish *(see page 178)*

To prepare the crust, blend the flour, sugar, and salt in a food processor until combined. Add the butter and while pulsing, cut in until the mixture resembles coarse meal. Add the egg yolk and wine, and pulse again. Mix just until moist clumps form. If the dough is crumbly, gradually add teaspoons of ice water until it comes together. Gather the dough into a ball. Flatten the dough ball into a disk. Wrap in plastic and chill for at least 40 minutes, and up to 2 days.

Position the rack in the center of the oven and preheat to 375°F.

Roll out the dough between 2 sheets of parchment paper to a 12-inch round. Remove the top sheet of the parchment paper and transfer the dough, along with the bottom parchment, to a rimmed baking sheet.

Place the pear slices, 1 tablespoon of the sugar, and the flour in large bowl. Toss to combine. Spoon the pear mixture into the center of the dough, leaving a 2-inch border. Using the parchment as an aid, fold up the outer edge of the dough over the edge of filling. Bake until the pears are tender, about 20 minutes.

Meanwhile, boil 1 cup wine, 1/2 cup water, and the remaining 1/2 cup of sugar in a medium saucepan until the syrup is reduced to 1/2 cup, about 10 minutes.

Reduce the oven temperature to 325°F. Drizzle half of the syrup over the filling. Continue baking the tart until the juices are bubbling thickly, about 20 minutes. Allow to cool.

Whisk 2 tablespoons of wine into the remaining syrup. Cut the tart into even wedges. Drizzle with syrup. Serve with a dollop of crème fraîche.

WINE PAIRING
Torii Mor Winery
2005 Late Harvest
Gewürztraminer

lemon tart
with white chocolate dipped blackberries

from Chef William King

The berries, dipped in melted white chocolate add a dramatic look to this rich, luscious lemon tart, and make it a special-occasion dessert, even though it is very easy to prepare. Big ripe Marionberries or loganberries are best, but given the variety of blackberries available locally during summer, you have many choices!

Makes 1 (9-inch) tart

For the tart crust pastry:
1 1/4 cups all-purpose flour
1/2 teaspoon salt
1 tablespoon sugar
8 tablespoons unsalted butter, very cold
4 to 5 tablespoons ice-cold water

Combine the 3 dry ingredients. Cut the butter into small dice, and cut into the flour mixture. Add the water, little by little, mixing only until the dough comes together. Flatten the dough into a disk, and wrap it in plastic. Refrigerate for 1 hour.

Remove the dough and roll into a 12-inch round. Lay it into a 1 to 1 1/2-inch deep, 9-inch loose-bottom tart shell, and press around the fluted edge. Freeze the dough.

Preheat the oven to 375°F.

Bring the prepared tart tin from the freezer and line the inside with foil. Add dried beans or rice to the foil liner to weigh down the pastry, and bake for 25 to 30 minutes.

Remove the foil and weights, and continue to bake for another 8 to 12 minutes, or until it is golden-brown all over. Allow the crust to cool.

For the lemon filling:
1 cup sugar
1/4 cup cornstarch
Pinch salt
1 1/2 cups water
1/2 cup freshly squeezed lemon juice
3/4 tablespoon grated lemon zest
6 large egg yolks
2 tablespoons unsalted butter

Combine all the ingredients, except for the yolks and butter. Simmer, whisking frequently, until thickened. Whisk in the yolks, one at a time, and continue to simmer. Add the butter, continuing to whisk at a simmer.

Remove from the heat, and pour into the baked and cooled tart shell. Allow to cool completely in the refrigerator.

For the blackberries and finished tart:
15 large ripe blackberries
4 ounces white chocolate
Fresh mint, for garnish

Melt the chocolate in a microwave oven, or over simmering water in a double boiler. Dip half of each berry and lay it on a plate. Chill until the white chocolate hardens.

Arrange the berries on the tart and garnish with fresh mint.

chocolate hazelnut brandy torte

from The Eyrie Vineyards

This Chocolate Hazelnut Torte recipe, created by Diana Lett, is as legendary in the Oregon wine community as the Eyrie 1975 South Block Reserve Pinot Noir. Diana often uses Eyrie Pinot Gris Grappa in place of the brandy for which the recipe calls. Hazelnuts and world-class chocolate make for a wonderful combination. This is a very crunchy, textural torte.

Serves 8 to 10

1/2 pound butter
1/2 pound Callebaut semisweet chocolate, or other fine chocolate
2 eggs
6 tablespoons sugar
1/2 cup (or so) good brandy
1/2 pound wheatmeal biscuits, coarsely crushed
Slightly sweetened whipped cream, for garnish
1/2 cup (or so) coarsely chopped dry-roasted hazelnuts, for garnish

Butter the sides of an 8-inch springform pan, and line the bottom with buttered waxed paper.

Melt the butter and chocolate together in a double boiler.

Beat the eggs and sugar together until foamy, and add the melted butter and chocolate. Add the brandy and crushed biscuits. Stir together gently, and pour into the paper-lined pan. Refrigerate overnight.

Unmold, peel off the waxed paper, and slice into servings. Garnish each serving with generous dollop of slightly sweetened whipped cream. Sprinkle with the chopped toasted hazelnuts and/or chocolate shavings, if desired.

vats and barrels

Much has been made of the materials that actually come in physical contact with wine through the final stages of production and storage—and with good reason as these materials can have a significant impact on what we drink and how it tastes. Today, vats for fermentation are most commonly made of stainless-steel. They are durable, easy to clean, and most importantly, inert—applying no flavor modification to the developing juice. In contrast, wooden barrels still prevail as the preferred vessels for storage during aging. An entire chapter could be written on the impact of oak on wine. In the spirit of keeping it simple, the winemaker determines the extent to which they want the oak's flavoring characteristic to be applied to the young wine. Oak barrels allow for very slow oxidation through its planks, but also imparts tannin and vanillin from the wood itself.

Some barrels are "toasted" while others are used new. Many winemakers are very particular about the specific forest from which the oak has come. All of these factors allow for individual and subtle distinctions and contribute to the "art" of the wine-making craft.

three berry shortcake

from Chef William King

WINE PAIRING
Rex Hill
2002 Maresh Vineyard
Late Harvest Riesling

I can't think of a better use for Oregon's beautiful cane berries than this simple but delicious shortcake that starts with support from old-fashioned cream biscuits and rich, heavy cream. It's the perfect summer dessert.

Serves 4

4 shortcake biscuits (recipe follows)
6 cups mixed blackberries, blueberries, raspberries
4 tablespoons sugar
6 tablespoons water
1 cup heavy cream

Toss the berries with the sugar and water, and allow to set and maserate for at least 1 hour.

Whip the cream until soft peaks can be formed. Sweeten if desired.

Split the biscuits and top with berries and cream. It can't be much easier than that!

Chef's note: I do not sweeten my whipped cream with sugar because I prefer it "as is." At times, I even use whipped crème fraîche or sour cream softened with a little heavy cream to add a bit of a tart "tone."

Shortcake Biscuits:
Makes 8 biscuits

1 3/4 cup all-purpose flour
1/4 cup sugar
1/2 teaspoon salt
1 tablespoon baking powder
1/2 cup unsalted butter, very cold
1 large egg
1/3 cup heavy cream

Preheat the oven to 425°F.

Combine the 4 dry ingredients. Cut the butter into small pieces, and cut into the dry mixture. Blend the eggs and cream together, and pour into the butter-flour mixture, and mix just until moist.

Turn the dough onto a floured surface, and knead just to pull it all together. Roll the dough to 3/4-inch thickness, and cut into 2 1/2 to 3-inch rounds with a biscuit cutter.

Place the biscuits on a parchment-paper-lined baking sheet, spacing them 1 inch apart. Bake for 12 to 15 minutes, or until browned.

Chef's note: If you like a "glossy" look to the top of the biscuits, brush with a little heavy cream just before baking.

chocolate mousse

from Spangler Vineyards

This is a classic light dessert created by Chef Carla Rutter, and is so easy to prepare. The orange reduction sauce will certainly impress your guests.

Serves 8

Mousse:
8 ounces chopped semi-sweet or bittersweet chocolate
4 tablespoons water
2 tablespoons brandy
4 tablespoons butter
4 eggs, separated
1/4 teaspoon cream of tartar
3 tablespoons superfine sugar

Place the chocolate and water in top of a double boiler over medium-high heat. Heat and stir until the mixture is melted and smooth. Add the brandy and butter, stirring until smooth. Set aside to cool slightly.

In a grease-free mixing bowl, beat the egg whites until soft peaks form. Mix in the cream of tartar and then slowly add the sugar, mixing briefly. Reserve.

Beat the egg yolks in another bowl until creamy and thick. Mix in the chocolate mixture and beat briefly.

Fold the egg-white mixture into the chocolate, folding in one fourth of the mixture at a time, into the chocolate, keeping it light and fluffy. Spoon into small dessert bowls and serve with orange reduction sauce (recipe follows).

Orange Reduction Sauce:
Juice from 2 oranges
Zest from 1 orange

Combine the juice and zest and reduce over medium heat by one-half. Strain to remove the pulp and serve as a garnish with the mousse.

"What is better than to sit at the end of the day and drink wine with friends, or substitutes for friends?"

—JAMES JOYCE

WINE PAIRING
Laurel Ridge Winery
1997 Finn Hill
Tawny Port

apple dumplings

from Chef William King

A baked apple stuffed with brown sugar, extra-sharp Cheddar, and toasted hazelnuts, blanketed in flaky pastry crust, served in a pool of vanilla cream and caramel sauce scattered with more toasted hazelnuts. Let's see… how can this not be heaven? It's a little bit of work, but well worth it. It makes a very dramatic entrance at the end of a special meal. You can also make this with firm pears, such as Bosc.

Serves 4

For the apples:
4 firm, crisp apples
Lemon juice, for soaking
1 cup toasted, peeled, coarsely chopped hazelnuts
1/3 cup brown sugar
1/2 cup grated Tillamook® Special Reserve Extra Sharp Cheddar cheese
4 tablespoons butter, still a bit cold, but softened
1/2 tablespoon cinnamon

Preheat the oven to 375°F.

Peel the apples and soak them in water with lemon juice to keep them from browning. Carefully core the apples, making the hole generous enough to hold the filling, but do not cut all the way down through the fruit. This will prevent the sugar and butter from running out of the bottom.

Combine the remaining ingredients, and blend well to form a paste. Fill the four cavities in the apples with the filling, and reserve in the refrigerator.

For the pastry:
1 2/3 cups all-purpose flour
1/4 teaspoon salt
1/2 cup plus 2 tablespoons butter, small cubes
2 ounces grated Tillamook® Special Reserve Extra Sharp Cheddar cheese
2 tablespoons cold water
2 large egg yolks

Combine the flour, salt, butter and cheese and blend until the mixture resembles coarse meal. Mix the water and egg yolk and add to the flour mixture. Gather the dough and form into two balls, being careful not to overwork the dough. Form the dough into two 6-inch discs. Wrap the discs in plastic wrap and refrigerate for at least one hour.

For the crème Anglaise:
2 1/2 cups milk
6 egg yolks
1/4 cup sugar

Scald the milk and let it cool. Mix the yolks and sugar with a wire whisk or electric mixer on low speed until thick and pale. Mixing constantly, slowly add the milk. Transfer the mixture to a heavy saucepan or double boiler and cook, stirring constantly. Do not let it boil.

When the custard is thick enough to coat the spoon, remove immediately from the heat to cool. (Speed the cooling process by placing the saucepan that the custard was cooked into a larger pan or bowl containing ice water.) Stir the mixture frequently as it cools to ensure a smooth texture.

To bake:
Divide the pastry into four equal portions and roll out to make approximately 8-inch circles. Place a chilled apple on each. Gather up the pastry and punch together at the top to form a pastry "package" around each apple. Trim excess. Bake until golden brown, about 20 minutes. Allow the apples to cool for 20 to 30 minutes before serving.

For the caramel sauce:
2 cups sugar
1 cup heavy cream
4 tablespoons butter

Caramelize the sugar by placing it into a sauté pan, and bringing it to a high heat. Within moments you will see the sugar turn to liquid and start to brown. Use a wooden spoon or wire whip to make sure the sugar colors evenly.

When it turns a dark brown, slowly add in the cream and butter. When mixed, remove from the heat.

To assemble:
4 to 5 tablespoons roasted, peeled, chopped hazelnuts, for garnish

Pour about 1/2 cup crème Anglaise on four serving plates. Place an apple on each. Drizzle the caramel sauce over the apples, and scatter the chopped hazelnuts over the apples and on the plates.

---

the first oregon wines list

In 1975, Ross Hawkins and Robert Parsons were working at Jake's Famous Crawfish Restaurant, and, wanting to find a way to introduce the "new" Oregon wines to the market, decided to create the very first Oregon wine list. Against everyone's advice, they contacted six Oregon wineries, and soon they had created a list of twelve wines. At first, the list was a source of amusement for some, however, within three years, Oregon wine sales accounted for nearly 40 percent of the total wines sales in the restaurant.

Today, their vision is supported by an interest in Oregon wines throughout the world, as restaurants from coast to coast, as well as in Europe, Asia, Australia and beyond, select Oregon wines to round out their international offerings.

the pantry

aïoli

1 clove garlic
3 egg yolks
1 teaspoon Dijon mustard
1 1/2 cup canola oil
1/2 lemon, juiced
1 teaspoon salt

Using a mortar and pestle, crush the garlic into a pulp. Add the egg yolks and mustard and mash into a paste. Once homogenous, begin to slowly drizzle in the oil. When all of the oil is incorporated, add the lemon juice and salt. Store, well covered in the refrigerator and use within 2 to 3 days.

Use a plastic squeeze bottle with a tip to control the stream of oil. If the aïoli begins to thicken, add 1 teaspoon of lukewarm water.

Chef's note: Since the eggs are raw, they must be certifiably fresh. If you are concerned about the threat of salmonella, use pasteurized eggs.

balsamic vinegar reduction

Pour one-half cup balsamic vinegar into a small saucepan. Bring to a boil and reduce the heat until the vinegar reduces to one-quarter cup, or turns into a slight glaze. Cool slightly. Pour into a plastic squeeze bottle. To decorate, drizzle the reduction on a plate. Refrigerate for later use. Bring to room temperature before using.

balsamic vinaigrette

2 tablespoons vinegar
1 tablespoon red wine vinegar
1 tablespoon Dijon mustard
1 tablespoon light brown sugar
1 clove garlic, minced
1/2 teaspoon salt
1/4 teaspoon freshly ground black pepper
3/4 cup olive oil

Whisk together the vinegars, mustard, sugar, garlic, salt, and pepper in a medium saucepan. Gradually whisk in the oil until smooth. If you are not using it right away, store in the refrigerator and whisk before serving.

clarified butter

Melt half a pound of unsalted butter slowly in a skillet or saucepan. After the butter is melted, let it sit while the foam and milk solids sink to the bottom of the pan. What is left on top is the clarified butter. Carefully pour the clarified butter out of the pot into a container, without allowing the milk solids to mix back in. The milk solids can be used to flavor steamed or sautéed vegetables.

Ghee, which may be found in Indian groceries and now in some supermarkets, is clarified butter that is totally shelf stable without refrigeration. However, if you make your own it is better to keep it refrigerated.

crème fraîche

1 cup whipping cream
2 tablespoons buttermilk

Combine the whipping cream and buttermilk in a glass container. Let it stand at room temperature (about 70°F) for 8 to 24 hours, or until very thick. Stir well before covering and refrigerate up to 10 days.

crêpes

1 cup all-purpose flour
2 eggs
1/2 cup milk
1/2 cup water
1/4 teaspoon salt
2 tablespoons butter, melted

In a large mixing bowl, whisk together the flour and the eggs. Gradually add in the milk and water, stirring to combine. Add the salt and butter; beat until smooth.

Heat a lightly oiled griddle or frying pan over medium-high heat. Pour or scoop the batter onto the griddle, using approximately one-quarter cup for each crêpe. Tilt the pan with a circular motion so that the batter coats the surface evenly.

Cook the crêpe for about 2 minutes, until the bottom is light brown. Loosen with a spatula, turn and cook the other side. Serve hot.

velouté sauce

1 1/2 cups white stock (veal, chicken or fish)
2 tablespoons unsalted butter
3 tablespoons flour
Salt
Freshly ground black pepper

Bring the stock to a simmer in a large saucepan. In a separate saucepan, melt the butter over low heat (don't let it burn) and add the flour. Raise the heat to medium and stir the butter and flour together for about 2 minutes. It should have a toasted smell, but do not let it get too brown, this is a roux.

Whisk the simmering stock into the roux (flour and butter mixture) and keep heating and whisking. When the stock begins to simmer again, turn down the heat to low and cook until the sauce thickens. If a thin skin forms, skim it away with a spoon. Depending on your stovetop, the sauce may take 5 to 10 minutes to reach your desired consistency.

Season to taste with salt and pepper.

Strain through a fine mesh strainer.

beurre blanc sauce

6 ounces white wine
3 ounces white wine vinegar
3 whole black peppercorns
1 shallot, quartered
1 cup heavy cream
6 ounces cold, unsalted butter, cut into pieces
3 ounces cold butter, cut into pieces

Combine wine, vinegar, peppercorns, and shallot in a saucepan. Reduce until the mixture is just 1 to 2 tablespoons and has the consistency of syrup. Add the cream and reduce again until the mixture is 3 to 4 tablespoons and very syrupy. Remove the pan from heat. Add the butter pieces, about 2 ounces at a time, stirring constantly and allowing each piece to melt in before adding more. (If the mixture cools too much, the butter will not melt completely and you will have to reheat it slightly.) Strain and hold warm on a stove-top trivet or in a double-boiler over very low heat until you are ready to use.

hollandaise sauce

1/2 pound unsalted butter, melted and warm, but not hot
3 egg yolks
1 tablespoon water
1 tablespoon lemon juice
Salt

Melt the butter and reserve. Combine the egg yolks and water in the top of a double broiler over hot, but not boiling water. Stir briskly with a wire whisk until the mixture is light and fluffy and the consistency of a light mayonnaise.

Remove the top of the double boiler from the heat, and slowly add the butter in a thin stream, while continuing to whip the mixture.

Season the mixture with the lemon juice and salt to taste.

béarnaise sauce

1/4 cup tarragon vinegar
3 sprigs fresh tarragon (or 1 teaspoon dried)
3 sprigs fresh chervil (or 1 teaspoon dried)
2 shallots, finely chopped

Combine the vinegar, herbs, and shallots over medium heat and reduce to approximately 1 tablespoon of thick paste. Allow to cool slightly. Add this paste to the hollandaise sauce (see above) in place of the lemon juice to create a béarnaise sauce.

cocktail sauce

1 cup purchased chili sauce
1/2 cup ketchup
2 tablespoons horseradish
1 teaspoon freshly squeezed lemon juice
1 teaspoon Worcestershire sauce
1/2 teaspoon dry mustard
1/2 teaspoon freshly ground black pepper
1 teaspoon Tabasco® sauce
1/4 teaspoon salt

Combine all ingredients and mix well.

tartar sauce

1/3 cup finely minced celery
1/3 cup finely minced onion
2 cups mayonnaise, homemade or store-bought
2 tablespoons freshly squeezed lemon juice
1 teaspoon Worcestershire sauce
2 tablespoons dill pickle relish
Pinch dry mustard
Pinch salt
Pinch pepper

Combine all ingredients and mix well.

pesto

2 cups fresh basil leaves, packed
1/3 cup pine nuts
2 to 3 cloves garlic, minced
1/2 cup extra virgin olive oil
1/2 cup freshly grated Parmigiano Reggiano or Pecorino Romano cheese
Salt
Freshly ground black pepper

Combine the basil and pine nuts in a food processor, and pulse. Add the garlic, and pulse a few times more. Slowly add the olive oil in a constant stream while the food processor is on. Pause, and using a rubber spatula, scrape down the sides of the food processor. Add the cheese, and pulse until blended. Season with salt and pepper to taste.

roasted tomato sauce

5 pounds Roma tomatoes
1/4 cup vegetable oil
1 cup diced yellow onions
1/2 cup diced celery
1/2 cup diced carrots
5 cloves garlic, minced
6 tablespoons olive oil
4 tablespoons butter
1/2 cup tomato paste
4 tablespoons freshly chopped basil
1 tablespoon dried oregano
1 tablespoon kosher salt
2 tablespoons freshly ground black pepper
1/2 tablespoon crushed red chili flakes

Preheat the oven to 250°F.
Slice each tomato into 4 to 5 slices. Arrange the tomatoes in a single layer on a foil-lined sheet pan or cookie sheet. Sprinkle the tomatoes with vegetable oil, and bake for 2 hours, or until slightly shriveled, but not dried out. Remove the tomatoes, chop them roughly, and set aside.
Sauté the onions, celery and carrots in the olive oil and butter over medium-high heat until soft. Add the garlic and continue to cook for 3 to 4 minutes. Add the roasted tomatoes, and the remaining ingredients. Simmer the sauce for 15 to 20 minutes over low heat.

seasonal accompaniments for roast chicken

Here are a couple of seasonal accompaniment options for roasted chicken *(see page 119)* that might be a bit different from the norm:

cheddar-chive bread pudding

8 ounces firm, dense bread, cut into 1-inch cubes
1 cup milk
1 cup cream
4 ounces shredded Cheddar, sharp is best
3 tablespoons freshly chopped chives
3 large eggs
1 egg yolk
1 teaspoon salt
1 teaspoon pepper

Preheat the oven to 325°F.

Combine all the ingredients in a large bowl, and toss well. Allow the bread to soak for 10 minutes. Pour into a lightly buttered (or pan-sprayed) shallow 2-quart baking dish or casserole. There will be extra liquid. Fill the pan to just below the top, covering all but the top edges of the bread.

Bake until the custard is set, and the top is browned, about 1 hour. I like to bake this one day ahead, cool, then refrigerate overnight. I cut it into portions and re-heat while the chicken is roasting. This produces crisp edges while retaining the creamy texture in the interior of the pudding. If you choose to serve the same day, allow the pudding to cool for at least 15 minutes before cutting.

green bean & tomato salad, and goat cheese with crostini

Salad
1/2 cup trimmed, blanched green beans
1 cup cut or diced assorted tomatoes
1/8 cup julienne-cut red onion
3 tablespoons extra virgin olive oil
3 tablespoons white wine vinegar
1 tablespoon Dijon mustard
1 teaspoon minced garlic
1/8 teaspoon each: salt, freshly ground black pepper, freshly chopped chives

Toss the vegetables together. Blend the remaining ingredients together to create a vinaigrette, and dress the salad.

Goat Cheese with Crostini
10 (1/4-inch-thick) baguette slices
Olive oil, to brush the bread
2 ounces fresh goat cheese
1 tablespoon mascarpone
1 tablespoon mayonnaise
Pinch salt
Freshly ground black pepper

Brush the baguette slices with olive oil, and toast under the boiler. Combine the remaining ingredients, and blend smooth. Arrange the crostini alongside the chicken, and mound the goat-cheese mixture on top of the crostini.

contributors

willamette valley

Adelsheim Vineyard
David & Ginny Adelsheim, founders
Recipe contributed by Chad Vargas, vineyard manager

Archery Summit
Erle Martin, president/CEO
Recipes contributed by Eric C. Maczko, executive chef (Pine Ridge Winery)

Bethel Heights Vineyard
Ted Casteel, Terry Casteel, Pat Dudley, Marilyn Webb, founders
Recipes contributed by Marilyn Webb

Chehalem
Recipes contributed by Harry Peterson-Nedry, founder & winemaker

Cristom Vineyards
Paul Gerrie, founder
Recipes contributed by John D'Anna, director of marketing and sales

Dobbes Family Estate
Recipes contributed by Joe Dobbes, founder & winemaker

Domaine Drouhin Oregon
Robert Drouhin and Véronique Drouhin-Boss, founders
Recipe contributed by Véronique Drouhin-Boss, winemaker

Elk Cove Vineyards
Pat & Joe Campbell, founders
Recipes contributed by Pat Campbell, and Travis Watson, vineyard manager, and Martha Wagner, director of retail sales and hospitality

Erath Winery
Dick Erath, founder
Recipe contributed by Tim McGinnis, cellar operations & maintenance

The Eyrie Vineyards
David & Diana Lett, founders
Recipes contributed by Diana Lett, and Jason Lett, winemaker

King Estate Winery
Ed King Jr. & Ed King III, founders
Recipe contributed by Michael Landsberg, executive chef

Lange Estate Winery and Vineyards
Don & Wendy Lange, founders
Recipe contributed by Wendy Lange

Penner-Ash Wine Cellars
Lynn & Ron Penner-Ash, founders
Recipe contributed by Ron Penner-Ash

Ponzi Vineyards
Dick & Nancy Ponzi, founders
Recipes contributed by Nancy Ponzi

Scott Paul Wines
Martha & Scott Wright, founders
Recipes contributed by Martha Wright

Sineann
Recipe contributed by Peter Rosback, founder & winemaker

Sokol Blosser Winery
Bill Blosser & Susan Sokol Blosser, founders
Recipes contributed by Susan Sokol Blosser

Stoller Vineyards
Bill & Cathy Stoller, founders
Recipes contributed by Bill & Cathy Stoller

Willakenzie Estate Winery
Ronni & Bernard LaCroute, founders
Recipes contributed by Paul Bachand, executive chef (Hunters Ridge Grill)
Recipes contributed by Gilbert Henry, executive chef & proprietor (Cuvée)

Willamette Valley Vineyards
Recipe contributed by Jim Bernau, founder

columbia gorge

Viento Wines
Recipes contributed by Rich Cushman, founder & winemaker

umpqua valley

Abacela
Earl & Hilda Jones, founders
Recipes contributed by Kiley Evans, winemaker

Brandborg Vineyard and Winery
Sue & Terry Brandborg, founders
Recipes contributed by Terry Brandborg

Reustle-Prayer Rock Vineyard and Winery
Stephen & Gloria Reustle, founders
Recipe contributed by Gloria Reustle

Spangler Vineyards
Pat & Loree Spangler, founders
Recipes contributed by Scott & Carla Rutter (Creative Catering)

rogue valley

EdenVale Winery at Eden Valley Orchards
Joseph H. Stewart, founder (1885)
Recipes contributed by Patrick Fallon, winemaker

RoxyAnn Winery
Jack Day, CEO
Recipes contributed by Michael Donovan, managing director

Trium
Rebecca & Randy Gold (Gold Vineyard), Laura & Kurt Lotspeich (Pheasant Hill Vineyard), Nancy Tappan & Vernon Hixson (Evans Creek and Venture Vineyards), founders
Recipes contributed by Chef Ryan Gabel

applegate valley

Wooldridge Creek Vineyard and Winery:
Ted & Mary Warrick, Greg Paneitz, Kara Olmo, founders
Recipes contributed by Kara Olmo

walla walla valley

Zerba Cellars
Cecil & Marilyn Zerba, Mark & Dana Retz, founders
Recipes contributed by Dana Retz

restaurants

The Dundee Bistro
Ponzi family, founders
Recipes contributed by Jason Stoller Smith, executive chef & partner

Joel Palmer House
Jack & Heidi Czarnecki, founders
Recipes contributed by Jack Czarnecki and Chris Czarnecki, chef de cuisine

Nick's Italian Café
Nick Peirano, founder
Recipes contributed by Carmen Peirano

Chateaulin Restaurant Français
Recipes contributed by David Taub, founder & chef de cuisine

sources

Apple Dumplings

Tillamook® Special Reserve Extra Sharp Cheddar Cheese, purchasing information available online at www.tillamookcheese.com.

Arugula with Truffle Vinaigrette and Truffle-Oil Coated Seastack Triple Cream Cheese

Oregon truffle oil is available from the Joel Palmer House, online at www.joelpalmerhouse.com.

Seastack cheese is available from Mt. Townsend Creamery, online at www.mttownsendcreamery.com.

Barbecued Buffalo Tri-Trips

Willamette Valley bison is available from L Bar T Bison Ranch, online at www.lbartbison.com.

Belgian Endive Salad with King Estate Pears, Blue Cheese, and Orange Champagne Vinaigrette

Rogue Creamery Blue Cheese is available from Rogue Creamery, online at www.roguecreamery.com.

Blue Corn Tamales with Serrano Ham and Goat Cheese

Blue-corn harinilla is a blue-corn flour appropriate for tamales. It is available from Los Chileros de Nuevo Mexico, online at www.888eatchile.com.

Cheese Service

Farmstead Smoked Gouda and French Prairie Brie are from Willamette Valley Cheese Company, purchasing information online at www.wvcheeseco.com.

Rogue Creamery Oregonzola is available from Rogue Creamery, online at www.roguecreamery.com.

Capricorn from Tumalo Farms available online at www.tumalofarms.com.

Chocolate Hazelnut Brandy Torte

Callebaut Semisweet Chocolate from Bernard Callebaut, purchasing information available online at www.bernardcchocolates.com.

Grappa of Oregon Pinot noir, purchasing available online at www.clearcreekdistillery.com

Crostini with Rogue Creamery Blue Cheese, Wildflower Honey, and Oregon Hazelnuts

Rogue Creamery Blue Cheese is available from Rogue Creamery, online at www.roguecreamery.com.

Duck with Edenvale Syrah

Rogue Creamery Blue Cheese is available from Rogue Creamery, online at www.roguecreamery.com.

Egg Noodles

All-purpose and Semolina flour is available from Pendleton Flour Mills, online at www.pfmills.com.

Garlic Glazed Pork Chops with Marsala Red Wine Reduction

Center-cut rib pork chops are from Carlton Farms, information about Carlton Farms pork can be found online at www.carltonfarms.com.

Lamb Ragu with Penne and Fresh Ricotta

Lamb shoulder is from Anderson Ranches, purchasing information available online at www.oregonlamb.com.

Northwest Bison Short Ribs

Southern Oregon bison is available from Full Circle Bison Ranch, online at www.fullcirclebisonranch.com.

Dagoba chocolate is available at www.dagobachocolate.com.

Southern Oregon polenta (along with other wonderful grains) is available from Butte Creek Mill, online at www.buttecreekmill.com.

The Classic Wines Auction

Information regarding The Classic Wines Auction can be found online at www.classicwineauction.com.

Jake's Famous Crawfish Restaurant

Information regarding Jake's Famous Crawfish Restaurant can be found at www.mccormickandschmicks.com.

Leadership in Energy and Environmental Design (LEED)

Information regarding Leadership in Energy and Environmental Design (LEED) can be found online at www.usgbc.org.

Low Input Viticulture & Enology, Inc. (LIVE)

Information regarding Low Input Viticulture & Enology, Inc. (LIVE) can be found online at www.liveinc.org.

Oregon Pinot Camp

Information regarding the Oregon Pinot Camp can be found online at www.oregonpinotcamp.com.

Oregon Wine Brotherhood

Information regarding the Oregon Wine Brotherhood can be found online at www.oregonwinebrotherhood.org.

Salmon Safe

Information regarding Salmon Safe can be found online at www.salmonsafe.org.

¡Salud! and The Oregon Pinot Noir Auction

Information regarding ¡Salud! and The Oregon Pinot Noir Auction can be found online at www.saludauction.org.

University Club of Portland

Information regarding the University Club of Portland can be found online at www.uclubpdx.com.

concordance

beef
boeuf bourguignon, 55
meatballs, 65
prime rib, 66
short ribs, 58, 67
steak, 59, 63, 149
tenderloin, 57
veal, 53, 61

beets
47, 48, 107

buffalo
bison short ribs, 113
tri-tips, 115

cheese
blue cheese, 8, 45, 111
feta, 157
goat cheese (chevre), 3, 17, 37, 47, 48, 57, 81, 180
Gorgonzola, 8, 163
Gruyère, 9, 11
Jack cheese, 27, 105
Mascarpone, 17, 180
Neufchâtel, 24
Parmesan, 11, 16, 17, 23, 99, 126, 145, 159
Rogue Creamery, 8, 45, 111, 138, 163
Roquefort, 8
Tillamook, 174
Tumalo Farms, 163
Willamette Valley Cheese Company, 163

chef william king
11, 15, 17, 19, 25, 41, 63, 71, 79, 85, 91, 97, 109, 112, 119, 126, 131, 132, 133, 145, 150, 155, 159, 163, 167, 171, 174

crostini
3, 5, 8, 37, 180

endive
43, 45, 48, 49

fig
111

hazelnuts
8, 19, 27, 41, 47, 111, 132, 169, 174

honey
8, 48, 71, 73, 109

varietals